- 2 X COMPLETE PRACTICE TESTS – PRACTICE LIKE THE REAL THING!
- WORKED EXAMPLE QUESTIONS ON EACH QUESTION TYPE, WITH SOLUTIONS AND EXPLANATIONS.
- STUDY HINTS AND TIPS TO MAXIMISE YOUR POTENTIAL

By
Kim Young

© COPYRIGHT 2020 - ALL RIGHTS RESERVED KIM YOUNG

The content contained within this book may not be reproduced, duplicated or transmitted without direct written permission from the author or the publisher.

Under no circumstances will any blame or legal responsibility be held against the publisher, or author, for any damages, reparation, or monetary loss due to the information contained within this book. Either directly or indirectly.

Legal Notice:

This book is copyright protected. This book is only for personal use. You cannot amend, distribute, sell, use, quote or paraphrase any part, or the content within this book, without the consent of the author or publisher.

Disclaimer Notice:

Please note the information contained within this document is for educational and entertainment purposes only. All effort has been executed to present accurate, up to date, and reliable, complete information. No warranties of any kind are declared or implied. Readers acknowledge that the author is not engaging in the rendering of legal, financial, medical or professional advice. The content within this book has been derived from various sources. Please consult a licensed professional before attempting any techniques outlined in this book.

By reading this document, the reader agrees that under no circumstances is the author responsible for any losses, direct or indirect, which are incurred as a result of the use of information contained within this document, including, but not limited to, — errors, omissions, or inaccuracies.

Contents

About this book 1

How to use this book 2

Exam secrets! 3

Key information on the LSAT 6

The sections of the lsat and details of the test 11

How many questions? 14

Results 15

LSAT score conversion 16

The important bits: the test sections, and how to ace them 20

How to take a practice LSAT 85

Test 1 91

Test 2 89

Answers 1 110

Answers 2 137

About this book

This book is a no-nonsense guide to acing your LSAT. I will teach you about the different question types, how to study, how to prepare on the day, how to score over 160 and get into the law school of your dreams. A lot of books have excess detail and boring content, but not this one! I have cut the fluff and made a fast-paced guide ready to help you get the most out of every second. I have included all the key details you need to give you the key ingredients to acing your LSAT.

I will not only teach you how to master each question type, but I will also show you how to maximise your efforts in studying, and in the exam room! So many students have the knowledge but underperform on the day, with my hints and tips you will get every point available to you for your knowledge.

It is best used as a study guide, read it, get the information that you need, and then study each sections of questions independently. Use my useful hints and tips on effective studying (proven by research) and then, when you're ready, attempt the practice tests.

I wish you the best of luck in your studies, and hope that this book gets you in to the law school that you desire!

How to use this book

You can't underestimate the importance of doing well in the high-pressure high-stakes environment of test day. How well you do on the LSAT will have a significant impact on your future- and I have the research and practical advice to help you execute on test day.

The book you're reading now is designed to help you avoid the most common errors test-takers frequently make.

I don't want to waste your time. My study guide is fast-paced and fluff-free. I suggest going through it a number of times, as repetition is an important part of learning new information and concepts.

First, read through the study guide completely to get a feel for the content and organization. Read the general success strategies first, and then proceed to the content sections. Each tip has been carefully selected for its effectiveness.

Second, read through the study guide again, and take notes in the margins and highlight those sections where you may have a particular weakness.

Finally, bring the Study guide with you on test day and study it before the exam begins.

Exam secrets!

This next section is all about how best to prepare for any exam, before and after, it's worth reading: get all the detail you need about preparing and how to act in an exam!

No time to hang about, let's look at how best to prepare for test and exams.

How Should I Prepare for Tests and Exams?

I spoke to the experts and have all the details on how to prepare for exams (of any kind!). You should treat the LSAT like a normal exam. Prepare effectively in the build-up to it and you will get the score that you need. So, without further ado, please check out my advice below.

Good Study Habits - what to do in the build-up to the exams.

1. Keep up with your work. If you attend class regularly, keep up with readings, and take notes conscientiously, studying can be a relatively pain-free process. Make sure to review and expand upon class notes regularly throughout the semester. Consider developing a glossary or collection of note cards for vocabulary review in each class. Many students find that preparing for an individual class for 60-90 minutes per day, five or six days per week, will leave them well-prepared at exam time.
2. Don't cram at the last second; Building off my previous statement, try studying for 60-90 minutes per day for a week leading up to an exam. All-nighters simply don't work for most people, and students experience declining returns on their efforts when they attempt to study for four and five hours straight.

3. Complete a mock test. Why not set aside an hour, and try to answer questions on a paper without using your notes? If you complete a mock test 3-4 days before an exam, you'll then know where to focus your studying. You may also combat pre-test jitters by demonstrating to yourself what you know. For the humanities, try answering a couple of potential essay questions on a timed, closed book basis and see how you do. Another simple way to conduct a mock test is to ask a friend or classmate to give you an oral quiz based on concepts in the textbook or in either of your notes.
4. Do not undertake multiple tasks while studying. Set time to study beforehand and follow through. This means leaving your dormitory room for most people and turning off visual/auditory distractions, including iPods, Facebook, and lyric music.
5. If you have any outstanding questions, go at least three days before the exam to see your teacher or tutor. You'll be able to go to office hours with an agenda if you've given yourself a mock test in advance.
6. Think about what written questions on the exam might be; outline every potential essay as a form of pre-testing and practice.
7. Find a group of other committed students to train with. A group study session is an ideal time for reviewing and comparing notes, asking each other questions, explaining ideas to each other, discussing the upcoming examination and difficult concepts, and delegating study tasks where appropriate. Set your group study session with an agenda and a specific timeframe, so that your work together is not off-topic.
8. Make sure you get lots of sleep. Dormant hours are often the time when we synthesize information completely, especially the topics that are covered in the few hours before bedtime. Once you take the test you want to be as new as possible to be able to fully engage your working memory.
9. Find ways to apply Class materials. Think about how course topics relate to your personal interests, societal issues and controversies, issues that have been raised in other classes, or different life experiences.
10. Develop a good routine 'morning-of' Eat a good breakfast. Go ahead and play something upbeat if the music gets you going. Get some physical exercise, even if it's a brief walk or stretch. If you feel nervous, record your anxieties on paper or use mental imagery to imagine doing something you enjoy and then apply those feelings to the exam. Think of preparing to a performance like an athlete before a contest or a musician.

11. Create an assault plan. Write down the key terms or formulas you need before you continue. Think how you are going to use the allotted time.
12. Carefully read out the directions.
13. Write a brief outline of the essay questions before beginning.
14. Use the elimination process on multiple-choice, matching questions. You may also want to cover the options first for multiple choice questions, and try answering the question on your own. Thus you will find the options for the answer less confusing. Make sure that you are aware of context, relationships and positionality between concepts, and multiple definitions of terms, as you prepare for multiple choice exams. A deep understanding of the vocabulary is a key to multiple-choice exam success.
15. Leave to the end the most time-consuming problems, especially the ones with low point values.
16. Concentrate on the matter at hand. If you do the test one step at a time, you will find it far less likely to be overwhelming.
17. If you're stuck on a question, bypass that question. Mark the question off so at the end of the exam you can get back to it.
18. If you have time at the end of the exam, go back and re-read your work and look again at multiple-choice questions. Check to see that you answered every question before you take the exam. But remember, your first answer is usually the best one. Be extremely careful about changing the answers later on.
19. Take a moment to review your test preparation strategy. Take into account what has worked and what needs to be improved. In particular, take a moment to see if your study group was helpful. If you feel that your test-preparation strategies need a job, go and see your professor or the Academic Advising Office.
20. Reward yourself, please. If you've been studying conscientiously for a week or more, you should take a little time to relax before you start your studies again.

Key information on the LSAT

This section will tell you everything you need to know about the LSAT, if you already know all this, skip to the question types and practice.

The more that you know what to expect, the more comfortable you're going to feel in your studies— and the more mental bandwidth you're going to have to focus on building the skills you're going to need to get a great score!

What is the purpose of the LSAT?

To be successful in law school and legal careers, you will need to demonstrate your ability to understand complex texts with accuracy and insight Organize and manage information and draw reasonable inferences from it. Think critically Analyze and evaluate the reasoning and arguments of others LSAT is designed to measure these skills.

The LSAT is a standardized collegiate examination, similar in design to the Scholastic Aptitude Test (SAT). It provides a standard measure of the verbal and reasoning skills deemed necessary for the legal profession.

While most law schools require the applicant to take the LSAT no later than December before the anticipated admission, those who test earlier have a greater opportunity to redeem themselves in the event of a low score. In most cases, applicants may take the LSAT up to three times in any two-year period. Be aware, however, that not all schools are strictly at the highest score— some average all scores together. So, unless your score is many points below your goal, it may not be in your best interest to repeat the test. Check the procedure used in any school that you apply to before you repeat the test.

If you are reasonably certain that you have crashed and burned in the test, you may also cancel your score entirely, provided that your written request to do so is received immediately (before grading). This will void all records of your having taken the test.

The test itself consists of five topical multiple-choice tests. Exams include Logical Reasoning, Reading Comprehension and Analytical Reasoning questions. An experimental section of one of these types of questions is also included for the purpose of field testing of future examination questions. The experimental section is not scored, but it is also not distinguishable from the sections scored. The sixth exam, writing sample, is also required and is not scored, but the text of the writing sample is sent along with the LSAT scores. Previously this was part of the exam, however you now have much longer to complete the writing sample after the exam day.

Questions on the LSAT are set up and administered by the Law School Admissions Council (LSAC), a non-profit organization established in 1947 to standardize, facilitate and improve the process of admission to law schools across the country.

Different multiple-choice sections of the examination (I will go into more detail later):

1. Logical Reasoning / Arguments: There are two sections of logical reasoning which are intended to test the applicant's ability either to draw reasonable conclusions from a valid argument or to detect flaws in an invalid argument.
2. Analytical Reasoning: also referred to as the Games section, this section checks the ability to track relationship structures throughout the written passage and properly account for the necessary parts under the conditions set.
3. Reading Comprehension: Precisely what it sounds like — this section measures how well you can read and understand various passages.
4. Variable: This is an ungraded portion and may be Logical Reasoning, Analytical Reasoning or Reading Comprehension. It's essentially used to try out new test things, but since you don't have a way to know which section is live and which isn't, you have to handle all sections as if they count against your ranking.

It is generally recommended that students take the LSAT before the beginning of the fall semester in December. Nevertheless, there are often advantages from taking the LSAT much earlier in the year; several experts suggest taking the LSAT in June or October, giving students more time to prepare. To this end, students have a wide range of preparation options available, including practical exams, private and online tutoring, and courses designed to refresh and instruct students in the content areas and skills needed to succeed in the LSAT. Due to the nature of the material and the amount of information that the students assimilate, LSAC recommends that all students prepare thoroughly before taking the LSAT, even if they have high confidence in their mastery of the material.

Test Day. You only need to have a few things with you on the test day. There are three things that students cannot do without:

the entrance ticket to the test center, without which the student cannot take the test; the current form of government approved photo ID (a driver's license or current passport is sufficient), without which the student will not be admitted; and three or four soft-leading 2 eraser pencils (no pens or mechanical pencils are allowed). Students must take their own no.2 pencils to the exam. The test proctor is not going to supply the pencils. It is permissible to bring in an analogue watch. No digital timepieces, watches or timepiece displays are permitted.

During the test period, students will leave at home or in their vehicles any materials not specifically mentioned on the approved material list. Identification For the purposes of the LSAT, valid identification is assumed to mean a card, badge or form that is A . issued by a government entity, B . recent, indicating that the identification has been issued in the last two years, and C . bears a recognizable photo of the applicant, along with the student's first and last name (both names must be shown on the identification document) and the student's last name. Due to recent revisions to the LSAC identity policy, only identifications that meet all three requirements will be recognized as legitimate IDs. Common forms of appropriate identification include driver's licences, passports, or other government-issued IDs. There are several forms of identification that will not be approved for the LSAT, and students must be mindful that they will not be admitted to the test center if they try to use an invalid form of identification. Such expired forms include out - of-date passports, LSAT tickets, student licenses, birth certificates, social security cards, family portraits, social insurance cards, photo credit cards, employee IDs, student IDs or any other form of identification that does not meet the three criteria set out above. Because LSAT is provided only on certain days, and since the student's delay in taking the test may adversely affect the fulfillment of the deadline for applications for scholarships or admission requirements, it is important that students have proper identification in the materials they carry to the test centre. It is highly recommended to put an alternate form of identification in a bag with the materials that the student brings to the test series. to expext on the test day The test day will begin with the student checking in before the test time has been allocated. For all examination periods except the June tests, students must report to the test center no later than 8:30 a.m.; for the June tests, students must report to the test center no later than

12:30 p.m. The student shall submit his / her admission ticket and an appropriate form of identification to the test center staff, who shall check the authenticity of the details on the list of registered students. Once verified, the test center staff will show the student to the test room and his or her assigned seat. The proctor will then supply the test materials. At the time of the assigned exam, registered students will be allowed to start the test.

After completion of the third section, the test proctor or center staff will announce a short break— usually 10 to 15 minutes in length— during which all test materials will be collected. Test materials must remain in the care of the test center staff during the break; students are allowed to walk around, stretch their legs, or use the bathroom. During the break, no cell phones or other electronic devices may be used, and students are not allowed to bring any food or drink back to the test area. Only those items brought to the test site in the previously described clear plastic bag are permitted under the LSAT Regulations. After the break, and after all the test materials have been returned to the appropriate students, the test will resume. Most students should expect to take approximately five hours to complete the test cycle, although this may vary from student to student.

Misconduct: Law School students should be informed that the LSAC has developed very strict rules on potential misconduct during the LSAT. Since lawyers are expected to adhere to a set of strict ethical standards, the application of the same high ethical standards applies to prospective law school applicants starting with the application process. The official LSAC statement in respect of the LSAT describes "misconduct" as: "the submission, as part of the legal process of admission to school, including, but not limited to, normal, transfer and visiting applications, of any information that is inaccurate, inconsistent or misleading, or the failure to provide information that may lead to a false or misleading inference, or the violation of any rule, shall be read as follows. Specific actions found to be wrongdoing by the LSAC include, but are not limited to, the following:

submission of an altered or fraudulent transcript submitting an application with incomplete, inaccurate or misleading details.

submission of a modified, false or improper letter of recommendation falsifiing documents impersonating another applicant in taking the LSAT. If a student is charged with wrongdoing, the LSAC shall immediately inform the school or schools concerned.

Pending findings and application kit details will be withheld until a member of the LSAC Misconduct and Irregularities in the Admission Process SubStore has had the opportunity to review the allegations. The LSAC has procedural rules concerning the management of harassment proceedings and instructions for the procedures to be used. These procedures shall begin once a representative has been assigned to investigate the allegation of misconduct.

Once the representative has concluded the investigation and has reached a preliminary decision, the findings of the representative shall be notified to the LSAC and the affected law schools and the decision shall be appended to the LSAT and LSDAS reports of the applicant. Other agencies and government bodies may also be informed, depending on the determination of the effect of the investigator. The LSAC has no authority to levy penalties or to advise and recommend disciplinary action. Disciplinary decisions are left entirely to the discretion of the schools concerned. Since allegations of misconduct may occur at any stage of the law school application process and extend beyond the academic period, any violation of the strict ethical standards of the legal profession may result in a range of penalties which may include:

In addition to the study and exam prep activities most students undertake before taking the LSAT, there are several basic steps that students can take to help maximize their test results: each test booklet has instructions on the front cover; read them carefully. Failure to follow the instructions may result in incorrect results or dismissal for failure to comply with them.

Read each question carefully. In many cases, the correct answer will depend on a complex understanding of the text, so it is important to be clear what is being asked for.

Please be sure to take the test at a measured pace. There are hundreds of questions that need to be answered. Spending too much time on a single question or passage may have a negative impact on the amount of time left to resolve other issues.

If the student finishes the test before time is called, it is advisable to go back through the test and review the answers. The student should use time to check the work and make corrections as necessary.

Score sheets are read by computer, so it is vital for students to ensure that their answers are neatly and with a minimum of smudging. If a mark is needed to be removed, the student must be confident that the mark is completely erased. Keep in mind that the marks and notes taken in the test booklets are not counted against your ranking, so make sure that all the responses are reported on the test sheet. Once an exam is called, students will put down their pencils and make no further marks on the board. Failure to do so will result in the examination being rejected and the score sheet being discarded.

The sections of the lsat and details of the test

The LSAT is divided into five individual subject examinations, covering a total of three areas of competence.

The content in each exam is broken down into the following categories:

Logical Reasoning–Students are evaluated for their ability to evaluate, critically analyze and complete a number of arguments.

Questions require the test-taker to read and understand a short passage, and then to answer questions about the passage in a manner that demonstrates logical and critical thinking processes. Examination passages require the student to identify the basic assumptions of the argument and other possible conclusions that may be drawn from it. In addition, the student will be asked to identify specific issues presented in the argument and to make parallel arguments that can be made, or to reveal supporting statements that either reinforce or weaken the argument. Both fields of expertise are provided by two independent exams.

Analytical Reasoning–Students are tested on the ability to analyze a table or collection of relationships between individuals and draw logical conclusions about the relationship.

The exam, also referred to as the Games section, is designed to measure the ability to objectively evaluate complex legal situations. The question structure of this section sets out a set of initial conditions, followed by a set of rules governing those conditions, and then encourages the student to draw up reasonable and logical conclusions on the basis of the situations, conditions and rules given. Follow-up questions may update or change an initial set of circumstances, rules or conditions requiring students to reorganize and draw up new conclusions.

Reading Comprehension–Students are tested for direct reading comprehension and identification of inferences on the basis of the material presented. The exam consists of several prose passages from different academic backgrounds, followed by a series of questions on the passage or selected sections of the passage. The examination calls on the student to draw conclusions based on an understanding of the primary argument and to locate specific information within the passages or to demonstrate an understanding of the overall structure of the selection process. Because reading skills such as identifying the main idea and knowing the causal relationship are being tested, the rote fact check is not included in the study.

Unscored portion–This segment is used to check possible future questions or new test formats. The grades of the unmarked segment are not included in the student's final test score. The section is not defined during the test, but is usually among the first three sections performed in order to avoid fatigue. The unsubstantiated segment can include questions covering any of the areas of expertise discussed in the standard LSAT course.

Writing prompt The writing prompt is a brief written exercise given after the exam. The question is not scored; instead, a digital copy is made and sent along with the test scores to the law schools that the applicant applies to. The written analysis consists of a prompt judgment, which presents a problem for the student to investigate, and a set of criteria that can be used to assess the issue and come to a conclusion. Students are required to write an essay using the parameters and to justify their decisions in writing. The problem that the student must analyze is generally a non-controversial issue that encourages dispassionate critical analysis and logical written argument. For a short time, the LSAC included an alternative type of prompt called the argument prompt— where a student had to analyze a logical argument similar to that seen in the logical reasoning examinations and criticize the argument— but that prompt was withdrawn as of June 2007. The prompt judgment commonly used for the written test represents the standardized procedure introduced at the beginning of the LSAT.

Students should be aware that while the writing prompt is included in the LSAT score, not all law schools place value on the writing exercise because it does not have a score. In any case, most law schools require a personal statement as part of the admission package.

However, many law schools place value on early writing, and the writing exam is assessed as a vital part of the LSAT for the majority of prospective law students.

How many questions?

Every part of the exam is allotted 35 minutes, including the written section. The number of questions may vary, but in general, each multiple-choice portion of the LSAT will have between 15 and 25 questions, depending on the nature of the passage and the difficulty of the questions asked. As a result, the average LSAT test-taker may expect to answer a minimum of 75 and a maximum of 125 questions over the period of the test day. Keep in mind that not only does the number of questions vary, but also the number of questions in each segment. While there are two sections of logical reasoning, the experimental section (which is not scored but is also not identified as such by the student) may be drawn from any subject in the regular exam series. As a result, two test-takers on the same day may experience large variations in the number and emphasis of questions raised during the LSAT series. Because scores are the same irrespective of what questions have been answered, students are strongly encouraged to familiarize themselves with the principles and activities of each subject area before taking the exams.

Results

Students who establish an electronic LSAT account will usually display their scores online within three to four weeks of the test. While most scores will be made available online at this time, there is no guarantee that scores will be posted within this timeframe.

The scores will be made available for testing no later than eight weeks. Students should also remember that online sharing of test scores will not have a speed advantage when reporting scores to law schools.

LSAT score conversion

There are three ways in which your LSAT score is presented:
1. Raw LSAT Score
2. LSAT Scaled Score
3. LSAT Percentile

Raw LSAT Score

Your Raw LSAT Score is just the number of questions you've got right with. Increasing LSAT will usually have between 100 and 103 questions, and your Raw LSAT score is between 0 and a limit of between 100 and 103. In computing your Raw LSAT Score there is no deduction for incorrect answers and all questions are weighted equally. It means that hard questions are worth as much as easy questions. LSAT Tip: When you run out of time skip some of the hardest questions and use the time you save to get more easy questions correct and increase your ranking.

LSAT Scaled Score

Raw LSAT Scores are converted into the LSAT Scaled Scores, which ranges from 120 to 180. So if you scored 0 on the Raw LSAT Score (0 questions right) you would likely have an LSAT Scaled Score of 120 and if your Raw LSAT Score was 101 you would likely have an LSAT Scaled Score of 180. The conversion process is done by using a statistical procedure called equating. Equating adjusts for the differences in difficulty between different LSAT tests. For example, the October 1997 LSAT was harder than the June 2007 LSAT and so if you wrote both tests and your Raw LSAT Score on both was 55 your LSAT Scaled Score for the June 2007 LSAT would be 149 and for the October 1997 LSAT it would be 150. Generally the same Raw LSAT Score will produce the same or very similar LSAT Scaled Scores. The Scaled Scores below converted from the raw score are approximate, for your exact scaled score refer to the scoring page of the LSAT you are scoring.

LSAT Percentile

A percentile rank is also reported for each LSAT score, reflecting the percentage of candidates scored below your test score reported. While the LSAT Scale Score is based on the specific LSAT test that you have written, the LSAT Score Percentile is based on the distribution of scores for the three-year period prior to the year in which the score is reported. Your percentile rank shows you that your score beats the average of weighted scores in the last three years. For example, if your LSAT Scaled Score is 157, you will have a percentile rank of approximately 75 percent, which means that your Scaled Score of 157 is better than 75 percent of the LSAT Scaled Scores for the last three years. The percentage scores below are for the period from June 2006 to February 2009. These include a statistical analysis of 429,816 LSAT scores over this 3-year period. The actual percentile rankings of your LSAT may vary slightly.

LSAT Score / Percentile Comparison Chart For example, use the table below if you scored 65 questions out of 101 questions on LSAT your LSAT Raw Score is 65, your LSAT Scale Score is 157, and your Percentile Score is 70.9 per cent. So while you got 65 percent of the questions right you're in the 70.9th percentile, your LSAT Scale Score was better than 70.9 percent of the people who wrote LSAT in the last three years. Remember that the table below is a reference and there will be slight variances with each writing of the LSAT. Table updated as of 4 March 2011.

For the most accurate results, convert your Raw Score to a Scaled Score on the conversion chart for your specific LSAT exam. Then convert the Scale Score to Percentile here.

Raw Score	Scaled Score	Percentile Rank
98-101	180	99.9%
97	179	99.9%
96	178	99.9%
94-95	177	99.8%
93	176	99.6%
92	175	99.4%
91	174	99.2%
90	173	99.0%
88-89	172	98.6%
87	171	98.0%
86	170	97.4%
84-85	169	96.7%
83	168	95.9%
81-82	167	94.6%
80	166	93.2%
78-79	165	92.0%
77	164	90.0%
75-76	163	88.1%
73-74	162	85.9%
72	161	83.4%
70-71	160	80.4%
68-69	159	77.6%
67	158	74.6%
65-66	157	70.9%
63-64	156	67.4%
61-62	155	63.9%
60	154	59.7%
58-59	153	55.6%
56-57	152	52.2%
55	151	48.1%
53-54	150	44.3%
51-52	149	40.3%
50	148	36.3%

48-49	147	33.0%
46-47	146	29.5%
45	145	26.1%
43-44	144	22.9%
42	143	20.5%
40-41	142	17.8%
38-39	141	15.2%
37	140	13.4%
35-36	139	11.4%
34	138	9.6%
33	137	8.1%
31-32	136	6.7%
30	135	5.6%
29	134	4.7%
28	133	3.7%
27	132	3.2%
26	131	2.5%
25	130	2.0%
24	129	1.7%
23	128	1.3%
22	127	1.0%
21	126	0.8%
20	125	0.7%
19	124	0.5%
18	123	0.4%
17	122	0.4%
16	121	0.3%
0-15	120	0.0%

The important bits: the test sections, and how to ace them.

Analytical Reasoning

Often referred to as "Logic Games," the Analytical Reasoning setups include 5-7 questions per scenario. Such questions are designed to test your ability to consider a set of facts and rules and to decide what might or should be accurate in the light of those facts and rules.

The skills tested are similar to those needed in law school and legal careers; as a lawyer, you will need to decide what might or should be the case, considering the set of rules, the terms of the contract or the facts of the case. That said, the situations in the theoretical logic portion of the LSAT are generally unrelated to the rule.

Beause's idea is to make these thought processes more available to a wide range of test operators.

The theoretical reasoning section lasts 35 minutes. During this time, you will encounter four facts patterns of conditions followed by 5 to 7 questions, for a total of 23 questions. So you've got about 8 minutes and 45 seconds to work through each set of questions. Fact trends pose situations with a set or two variables that I call counters — people, dorm rooms, positions around an office table, stuff like that— and add rules that govern how to use them. Questions test your ability to apply the rules and make deductions, which (believe it or not) is a skill that you use a lot in law school and law practice.

The thinking processes involved in applying the law and case law to a scenario are not very different from the thinking and method involved in applying the rules to the facts in the context of analytical reasoning problems. In fact, attorneys concentrate on arcane law for a long period of time, and the LSAT shows whether you can maintain that kind of attention to detail for an extended period of time. So, while working analytical reasoning problems will not be part of your grueling first year of law school, you need analytical skills and attention to detail these problems test to withstand the Socratic teaching methods that your law professors that apply In the following sections, I will break down the question types contained in this section. First, though, it is worth looking briefly at the shape that these problems will take on the LSAT.

Unlike problems in other areas, Analytical Reasoning problems will test the ability to wade through a lot of information, think quickly under pressure, and keep pace. On top of that, this segment, more than any other, will allow you to define and keep a tab running on the relationship between various bits of information across different points of convergence. (On the other hand, this is the only part of the LSAT where the test taker can make sure that their answer is correct.) Most examines hate this portion of the LSAT, forcing you to keep track of a lot of information and interactions between the different bits of information. And there's no denying it could be quite frustrating. But one thing you will find by practicing the problems ahead of time is that one or two of the Analytical Reasoning problem forms will be easier for you to understand and complete, relatively speaking, while others will be more challenging. Particularly because you will be testing under time-sensitive, high-pressure conditions, it is advised that you first work out the problems that come to you more quickly, and then go back to complete those that take more time.

Remember, if your experimental segment turns out to be Analytical Reasoning, you'll need to approach all sections as if they were actual, because you don't have a way to know which one will be scored and which one won't. Just note, you're not penalized for the amount of wrong answers, so when time is short, guessing is a much better strategy than leaving questions unanswered.

Of course, it is important to study for all three parts of the LSAT, but taking the time to learn how to understand and solve Analytical Reasoning games will be the easiest way for most people to significantly improve their performance. That's because the other two parts evaluate the skills that people actually use on a regular basis. It is definitely possible to improve a person's reading comprehension and/or logical reasoning skills, but most people taking LSAT will already be very good in these two fields. There's certainly an upside potential, but it's a little limited. Nevertheless, the problems in Analytical Reasoning need less widely used skills, so the upside potential of learning the skills needed to solve these kinds of problems is immense.

Key to Success in the Analytical Reasoning Section In the Analytical Reasoning section of the LSAT, the challenges are in the form of what the LSAC calls setups. Each setup consists of two main parts. The first is the elements— these are the sets of people (the most common), places, or things. The second is the conditions–the constraints under which the elements operate, the limits on how they can be manipulated. Most people refer to the conditions as rules or clues; in this sense, the three terms are interchangeable. To answer questions after the setup, you will need to organize, identify, group or otherwise manipulate the elements in accordance with the constraints.

because each system will have multiple elements and different rules, some of which apply to all the elements and others which apply only to some of the elements, it will be nearly impossible to answer all 22-24 questions in the Analytical Reasoning segment in the 35 minutes allotted by trying to figure out the answers in your mind. In reality, attempting to do so is probably the one thing that has the biggest negative impact on the average person's LSAT score.

Trying to get the answers in your head will pull your score down in two ways. First of all, it is very unlikely that you will be able to answer all the questions without guessing. You're just not going to have time. Odds are high that you're either forced to leave a lot of the questions blank or just take random guesses because you're running out of time. While wrong or blank answers won't lower your score on their own, each of them is a question that you might have answered correctly if you'd used a more effective strategy. In other words, while there is no penalty for an incorrect or missing answer, each is a missed opportunity to raise your score.

Second, even in those cases where you spent a lot of time thinking about the question, some of your answers are very likely to be wrong, because it's extremely difficult to mentally solve these problems. In fact, the key to success in the Analytical Reasoning section of the LSAT lies in understanding that it is not a test of pure reasoning by any part of the imagination. In addition, your success in this section depends not only on your reasoning skills, but also on your ability to quickly make accurate visual representations of complicated written information. In fact, this latter skill is probably even more important than the former. In other words, Analytical Reasoning is just as much a diagram test as a rationale test, if not more so. Of course, LSAC can't come out and call this section Rapid Diagramming, because it doesn't sound as exciting (or almost as intimidating) as Analytical Reasoning.

We said earlier that this is the only section where you can be 100% sure that your answer is correct. This is because if you draw a diagram correctly, you can simply look at your diagram and visually confirm the correct answer. I Also said that although the Analytical Reasoning section of the LSAT is the one that seems to be the most intimidating, it is also the section that offers the most room for improvement to increase your potential score. If you're like an average person, the ability to visualize these kinds of problems begins with what's basically a zero baseline. If you are only slightly good at diagraming Analytical Reasoning configurations, you should expect a significant increase in your future LSAT ranking. When you take the time and effort to make it very good, the effect on your ranking will be tremendous.

Not everyone who takes the LSAT is capable of achieving the highest score. Nonetheless, several people who are actually worthy of ranking in the top percentiles of test-takers struggle to do so, and end up with a poor score–one that's nothing to brag about, and isn't good enough to get them into the best schools, let alone earn any scholarship money. For most of these aspiring lawyers, the key reason they did not achieve the high score they were capable of was poor performance in the Analytical Reasoning section.

Analytical Reasoning Made Simple-Analytical reasoning problem sets differ in the subject. You may be asked to perform a rather dumb job, such as selecting toppings for ice cream flavours, or you may find yourself taking on the role of city planner, designing buildings on a new construction site. Irrespective of their subject matter, all analytical reasoning problems are dealt with in much the same way.

Read the facts of the matter.

Every logic game presents a scenario with a paragraph or two that shows whether the problem involves ordering or grouping, lists the variables (playing pieces) and otherwise provides the details you need to set up a diagram that I call the counter map.

Analyze the rules, please.

Also referred to as conditions, the rules set limits on the organization or grouping of counters on the counter map.

Answer the questions, please.

After you have studied the consequences of the rules and documented them and their corollaries on your counter map, you have laid the foundation for tackling the issues that follow.

Get the facts, decide between ordering and grouping, and set up your counter map The first sentence of the logic game sets out the facts. When you read the information, complete these tasks: determine whether a logic game is a problem of ordering or grouping.

The basic distinction between them is that ordering problems allows you to position the counters in relation to each other, and grouping problems ask you to bring the counters together in two or more sets.

List the initials of the items you need to order or group. These are the pieces of your game. Every aspect always begins with a different letter, so referring to the first part is quick and easy. You only have the space in your test booklet to build your counter map, so write compactly.

Build the basis for your counter map. The most popular counter map for logic games is a very simple box chart with the locations or group names as column headers, below which you place the counters according to the rules, then interpret the rules and change the counter map. The second half of the logic game is a set of conditions that determine how the counters can be organized or grouped. Some rules allow you to place the counter in a permanent place on the counter map. We're calling these target rules. An example of the target rule is, "Gary is the last scheduled one." Unfortunately, very few rules in LSAT logic games are targets. Many point to where the counters don't belong, such as, "Gary isn't scheduled last." Some give you information about where the pieces belong relative to each other, such as, "Lucy is scheduled before Marco." Others tell you something is true about a counter, based on when the situation is true for another counter, such as, "When Marco is scheduled before Penelope, Harriet is scheduled to play. Shortcuts save time and space and encourage you to return to the rules simply by looking at your counter map. Different types of rules call for different recording methods, and rules for ordering games may be worded a little differently from those for grouping games.

Your rule shortcuts don't have to be fancy as long as you consistently use them. Several popular shorthand symbols include: the arrows to mark the spatial relationship between the pieces= or the arrows to mark the positive or negative relationship between the pieces A slash through a letter to show that a piece can not be in one position or do something underscores) (to label spaces that must be filled with unknown parts.

Or just come up with your own shorthand, no matter how much you know it works!

Then you need to answer your questions.

Building a logic counter map is important, but you don't get points unless you answer questions. Most of the questions you experience in this section fall into four types: possible listing / assignment questions: almost all logic games begin with a question that asks you for an answer that provides a possible listing (order problems) or assignment (grouping problems) of the counters.

Quantity Questions: In order to answer these questions, you usually determine how many counters should occupy a particular position, so that they are most common in ordering-problem sets.

Questions to add-a-rule: Most questions provide an additional provision to be used to answer only that question.

Open questions: this type of question simply asks what is true, false or conceivable on the basis of the original conditions.

How to draw your diagram: Essentially, your diagrams will consist of three things: rows (including simple circles, boxes, and tables), symbols, and setup elements names. Once you have resolved a setup question, you can keep the basic diagram for the rest of the questions for that setup, but sometimes you will have to delete most of the names and then rearrange them on the diagram for each question.

Rule Breakers. Each issue gives you some known information. These are the rules you've got to work with. Rule breakers are options that are directly in conflict with the law and can be easily ruled out.

Example: John sits next to Bob.

It's a rule. So any seating arrangement that doesn't have John sitting next to Bob is a rule breaker, and it's incorrect. Quickly scan through the list of responses and delete all those that have Bob and John sitting apart.

Example: Mary isn't sitting next to Bob.

Here's another law. Quickly scan back through the option of answers and delete all that Mary and Bob have together. For every rule that is given, check quickly and see if there are any answers that immediately break the rule and eliminate it.

Scratch Paper: Use your text booklet extensively as a scratch paper. This is a great ally! If you have finished the Analytical Reasoning portion without scribbles within, you have not taken advantage of all your potential resources. A good diagram or drawing of the problem described is a great help when it comes to solving the problem.

Be warned, though, that when you create your drawings, you'll need to be efficient. Don't waste time filling in more of the details you need. That's why the symbols are great tools. They're going to save time and effort. Don't include any useless information on your diagram or spend time making it pretty. Only fill in what is clearly stated, or what you can easily deduce. Focus on getting the bare essentials down on paper and spend your time trying to solve the problem more productively.

Tough Questions: If you're stuck with a question or it seems too hard or too complicated, don't waste time. Move on, remember though, if you can quickly check for obvious rule breakers, the chances of guessing correctly will be greatly improved. Once you give up entirely, at least check out the simple rule breakers, which should take out a few possible answers. Eliminate what you can, and then guess the rest of it before you move on.

Always accept a situation of face value in the problem. Don't think too much about it. The LSAT makers are not trying to throw you away with a cheap trick. If the configuration says there are six seats in a row, you can be sure that there is a single row of files and that one person is sitting next to the next person and there are two ends to the row. Don't overcomplicate the problem by creating imaginary scenarios that warp time or space. These are normal problems with resolvable answers. It's just that all the knowledge isn't readily apparent, and you've got to figure it out.

Read the description of the problem carefully. Don't miss the question because you have misunderstood the description of the problem. The definition is there because it is important to understand the problem. Don't waste too much time. You need to read it carefully and efficiently.

Rules are often loose or tight. Don't confuse the two when you're hunting for rule breakers. A loose rule gives vague details of the issue. A tight rule gives specific details of the issue. Tight guidelines are much more useful because they provide more detail, making it easier for you to make clear decisions about answering choices.

Example: Loose: Bob is standing behind Joe. Tight: Bob is standing right behind Joe.

Don't deceive the answer that Bob has two spaces back from Joe, if only the loose rule above is given. If you have a loose rule, you can only exclude the option of answer that Bob has in front of Joe.

Double negatives can be considered as positive. If the choice of a law or answer has two negatives, mentally turn it to a single positive.

Example: He's not going to be out there. He's going to be out there.

Response Selection

Eliminate choices as soon as you realize they are wrong. But be careful, though. Make sure you consider all possible answers. Just because one looks right, it doesn't mean that the next one isn't going to be even better. Take a second to make sure that the other choices are not just as obvious. Don't make a hasty mistake about that. There are only two times you need to stop before you consider any other choice of answer. The first is, if you are absolutely positive, that the choice of answer that you have chosen follows all the laws. The second is when the time is almost out, and you've got to make a quick guess.

Don't panic if you're caught between two options of answers that seem different. After eliminating the other three, the odds of answering correctly are now 50/50. Play the odds instead of wasting too much energy. You're guessing, but you're wisely guessing, because you've been able to do away with some of the answers that you know are wrong. If you're removing options and find that the option of answer you're left with is obviously also incorrect, don't panic.

Selection Problems

For the Analytical Reasoning section, a universal must-do is to pay careful attention to the conditions laid down for the problem; the problems of selection are no exception. There are a number of facts that you will find out about each player under the circumstances, as well as what each player may or may not do, how they can and can not be linked—in other words, strict guidelines for how they work. Selection problems require you to pay special attention to this information because you will be using it to take smaller groups out of the main one.

The issue criteria can look like this: Amy has to pick three employees to go to the junket.

To order to identify problems such as this, you will need to consider the following aspects: who must be selected according to the criteria specified Who is eligible for selection Who is not eligible for selection If certain particular players are selected, which other players must or must not be selected? After analyzing the facts, how many players are actually eligible The following example should help to explain the following concepts: there are six siblings attending the same college. They're Naya, Chris, Maggie, Elliott, Joel, and Petra. Five classes are scheduled for the next term, which they may attend, subject to the following restrictions: if Joel registers for a particular class, then Petra does not register for the same class. When Naya signs up for a particular class, Chris doesn't sign up for the same class. When Petra signs up for a particular class, either Maggie or Elliott can sign up for the same class, but not both. When Chris does not sign up for a class, neither Maggie nor Petra will sign up for that class.

As you can see, there's a lot to keep track of right from the start. You can see why drawing a diagram is needed to solve these problems. Diagrams make it easier to refer to those links when addressing a series of questions, each of which generates a slightly different category and can speed up the response time.

Given the set of conditions set out above, try the following question: if Naya enrolls in a particular class, what is the maximum number of other siblings who may also attend that class?

As you can see, drawing up a link when you first read through the conditions will prevent you from having to waste precious time checking the conditions for each additional question.

The task questions will look quite similar to the selection questions. In both cases, you will be asked to select individuals from a larger group on the basis of the conditions stated. The primary difference is that when it comes to selection issues, you will identify players from a larger group and discard the rest of them for the purposes of that question. However, when assigning problems, you must select and assign each player identified to one group or another–there are no wallflowers in assignment problems.

The following example should be used to illustrate the difference: Selection problem There are six siblings attending the same class. They're Naya, Chris, Maggie, Elliott, Joel, and Petra. Five classes are scheduled for the next semester, which they may attend, subject to the following restrictions:

If Naya enrolls in a particular class, what is the complete list of the siblings who may also attend that class?

Assignment Problem There are six brothers and sisters attending the same class. They're Naya, Chris, Maggie, Elliott, Joel, and Petra. Two classes, the green and the yellow ones, are scheduled for the same weekdays and hours. Each of the brothers and sisters will enroll in one of the two schools. All the brothers and sisters listed above may participate, subject to the following conditions:

Which of the siblings is going to enroll in the green class?

It should be immediately obvious that the primary difference between the two problems is that the problem of assignment requires that each person be accounted for and assigned a slot in one group or another. While the same skills used in selection problems can be used to solve assignment problems, many testers consider assignment problems harder to solve. Because all teams have to be put in a squad, there are fewer loose ends. This makes it easier for the examiner to be accountable to everyone and to ensure that something has not been missed. For this reason, given the additional step, many people prefer assignment problems to selection problems.

- Determine which players are expected to be in a given group.
- Determine which players can be included in a given group.
- Determine the number of players to be grouped into a specific category.
- Determine which players are not qualified for inclusion in a given group.
- Determine should players must or must not be matched with other specific players.

Connection game problems are similar to assignment problems in that they require you to place each of the players listed in a group based on the specified conditions. With connection game problems, however, you must do this on the basis of the connections or characteristics of the different players as defined in the set conditions: you are connecting the players to those characteristics.

There's a lot going on, so it's good to start by breaking the problem down into smaller, more manageable parts. The following systematic progression works well in sorting out the problem before tackling the issues: start by listing the different players. Players are often identified in a consecutive series, which makes it pretty easy.

Identify and note the different characteristics that are appropriate for the different players.

Where appropriate, the various characteristics of the players must be balanced. Possible characteristics are sometimes reported in the negative (in an attempt to confuse the LSAT tests). For example, it could be said in the same way: all players who have Characteristic Y can not have Characteristic Z. Consider the following example and implementation of the above steps: there are four students: Maria, Brandon, Charles and Donita. Those students do not like the following classes: algebra, biology, and P.E., which are consistent with the following: each student does not like at least one of the classes; no student does not like all three classes; at least two, but not all four, students do not like biology; if Brandon does not like a class, then Donita also does not like that class; if a student does not like biology, then that student also does not like algebra.

From reviewing the above example, it's easy to see how you can get your wires crossed as you go deeper into the issues (which can build on each other).

So, to apply the above steps, I first list the players: Anna, Brandon, Charles, and Donita.

Next, you take note of the different characteristics that are, in this case, the classes that students do not like. Consider the traits that are directly attributed to a particular player (Charles does not like algebra) as well as those that are implicitly attributed to a player (if Brandon does not like a class, Donita does).

- Once you've done so, you're ready to face the types of issues that will be related to linking games issues, such as: Determine which players must have a particular feature.
- Determine which players might have a special feature.
- Determine which players should certainly not be related to a particular feature.
- Separate which players must, must not or may not be associated with the same characteristics as other players.

Skipping Problems: Some Advice

Due to the difficulty level faced in Analytical Reasoning, some students make a strategic decision to skip some of the problems in this portion of the LSAT in order to have more time to focus on fewer questions, potentially increasing the number of questions they answer correctly. This is a common strategy, and given the way the LSAT is scored and the severe time constraints of the Analytical Reasoning section, it can make a lot of sense to follow it. In other words, since you don't have enough time to give all the questions the attention you need to answer them, and since the LSAT score is based solely on correct answers, it is quite reasonable to devote more time to a lower number of questions if it leads to more questions being answered correctly.

If you decide to use this strategy, it is important for you to know that not all the LSAT Analytical Reasoning questions are of equal difficulty. They're all challenging, of course, but some are less difficult than others, while some are more difficult. So which ones are you going to miss, and which ones are you supposed to concentrate on? Well, while some people may not agree, most test takers find that assigning setups is the hardest, ordering setups is the least difficult, and grouping setups fall somewhere in between. Also, you're not supposed to skip the first setup, as it's never the toughest one on the exam.

Another important consideration is that, generally speaking, configurations with more criteria are typically easier to answer than those with fewer rules. It might seem that the opposite would be true. This is probably due to the fact that reading and understanding more rules takes more time than reading and understanding fewer rules. They say appearances are often misleading, and in this case they are correct. It's not reading and interpreting the rules that will take most of your time in the Analytical Reasoning section; it's thinking about how to get the correct answer. The more information you have to begin with, the less you have to sort out in order to find the right answer. Therefore, when it comes to resolving problems efficiently, the more circumstances, the better.

The Supermarket shall reduce precisely five of the eight products— G, L, M, N, P, R, S, and W — in compliance with the following conditions: if both G and S are reduced, W is also reduced.

When N is reduced, neither R nor S shall be reduced.

When P is reduced, L shall not be reduced.

Of the three areas L, M and R, two are to be reduced.

Question 1 If both M and R are reduced, which of the following areas is a pair of areas none of which could be reduced?

    A: G L
    B: G S
    C: L G,
    D: L P
    E: P G,

Question 1 This question concerns the decision of the Store to minimize spending in five out of eight regions. The question requires you to conclude that M and R are among the areas that need to be reduced, and then to decide which pair of areas may not also be among the five areas that need to be reduced.

The fourth condition set out in the passage on which this problem is based involves the reduction of exactly two of M, R and L. As the question asks us to conclude that both M and

R are reduced, I know that L must not be reduced: reduced: M, R Not reduced: L The second condition implies that, if N is reduced, neither R nor S is reduced. So both N and R can not be reduced. Here, since R is reduced, I know that N can not be. Thus, adding this to what I have determined so far, I know that L and N are a pair of areas that can not be reduced if both M and R are reduced: Reduced: M, R Not reduced: L, N Answer choice C . is therefore the correct answer, and you are done.

If you are taking the test, if you have decided the correct answer, there is no need to rule out any other choice of answer. Nonetheless, for correctness it is worthwhile taling a look at the wrong answers. For this question, any incorrect choice of answer can be ruled out by finding a possible outcome in which at least one of the two areas indicated in that choice of answer is reduced. Consider the answer choice A ., which lists the pairs G and L. I already know that for this question, L must be one of the areas that is not being reduced, so all I need to consider is whether G can be one of the areas that is being reduced. Here is one possible outcome: reduced: M, R, G, S, W If areas M, R, G, S, and W are reduced, then the assumption for the question holds and all the conditions in the passage are met: both M and R are reduced, as is assumed for this question.

Both G and S are reduced, and W is also reduced, so that the first condition is satisfied.

N is not reduced, therefore the second condition is not relevant.

P is not reduced, therefore the third condition is not relevant.

The exact two of L, M, and R are of, so the fourth condition is fulfilled.

Therefore, because G could be reduced without breaching the conditions, the choice of response A . can be ruled out. Therefore, since G appears in the pair indicated in the option of answer B ., I can also see that B . is wrong.

Now consider the solution option D ., which lists the pairs L and P. I already know that for this issue, L must be one of the areas that is not being reduced, so all I need to ask is whether P can be one of the areas that is being reduced. Here is one possible outcome: reduced: M, R, P, S, W If areas M, R, P, S, and W are reduced, then the expectation for the question holds and all the conditions in the passage are met: both M and R are reduced, as is assumed for this question.

G is not reduced, therefore the first condition is not important.

N is not reduced, therefore the second condition is not important.

P is reduced and L is not reduced, so that the third condition is satisfied.

The exact two of L, M, and R are of, so the fourth condition is fulfilled.

Therefore, because P could be reduced without violating the conditions, the option of response D . can be ruled out. Furthermore, since P appears in the pair indicated in the choice of answer E .,I can also see that the choice of answer E . is incorrect.

This question was of moderate difficulty, based on the number of test participants who answered it correctly when it appeared on the LSAT. Response E . was the most frequently chosen incorrect response option.

Reading Comprehension

You will see one portion of Reading Comprehension graded on Test Day, which means that Reading Comprehension makes up around one quarter of your total points.

Duration: 35 minutes Length: 26-28 passage-based questions (divided into 4 reading passages).

Subject matter: Four parts are taken from four fields: Law, Social Sciences, Technology and Humanities. Three of the passages are going to ask you questions about a single text. One of the passages, known sometimes as the "Comparative Reading set", will feature two texts, and the questions will focus on how they relate to each other. The basics A Reading Comprehension task is made up of these parts: 1-2 passages: Total length of the text will be about 50-60 lines. The topics are diverse, and many may be unfamiliar to you. Questions: You'll be asked several questions about the text. Some of the questions can be answered with information explicitly stated in the passage, but many questions ask about what can be inferred. Choices: You'll be presented with five choices. Only one of them is correct. You'll see us refer to the correct choice as the "answer" throughout your practice sessions. How to answer the Reading Comprehension section most effectively? The first read—focus more on the main claims than the details: The overall point of a passage is much more important than the details the author uses to support that point. High scorers read critically, identifying the purpose of each paragraph as they go along. In fact, it's often the case that the longer someone spends reading and re-reading for details, the worse they perform on Test Day. Pay attention to structure: Instead of focusing too much on what is being said ("What is it about?"), focus on why it's being said ("What is the point?"). Ask yourself questions as you go along: Why did the passage's author include this quote? Was it supporting a claim? Why did the author include this example? What role does each claim, each paragraph play in the text's overall argument? Strong critical readers ask themselves how—and why—the argument is being built. What is the author doing?

Pay attention to opinions: As a law student and as a lawyer, you'll need to be able to keep track of assenting and dissenting voices. Where do they overlap? Where do they diverge? If you see an author's (or critics' or anyone's) point of view expressed in the passage, take note! You will almost certainly see questions about the different perspectives. Understand the task: Different questions require different kinds of work. For example, recognition questions that ask you to recognize details from the passage call for a close re-reading of the relevant part of the passage. In contrast, main point questions are best answered without close re-reading.Irecommend different approaches for different question types—find out more in the practice area ofMysystem. Take time to think: For some question types, it helps to try to predict what the answer is likely to be before looking at the choices—this can help you locate the answer quickly. For other question types, it's not as easy to make a prediction, but you should still stop to think about the task. If you don't take the time to think and prepare, it's all too easy to get lost in the choices. Students who find themselves reading and re-reading without a clear purpose are more easily distracted by wrong choices. Evaluate the choices: Once you set yourself up for success, either by making a prediction or by gaining control of your task by clarifying it in your own words, it's time to evaluate the choices. Ask, for example, "Does this choice match my prediction?" or, "Does this choice accurately restate a detail I just located?" All Reading Comprehension questions are not created equal! You are likely to find some passages more challenging than others, due to the density of the text, your familiarity or comfort level with the topic, or the complexity of the questions. Be prepared for a diverse array of challenges, and remember that it's completely acceptable to skip a few questions in order to make sure you have the time to consider all four passages. Dos and Don'ts Here are some ideas to keep in mind as you begin to develop an approach that works best for you on the Reading

Comprehension section:

Don't try to read faster: LSAT Reading Comprehension isn't about speed and memorization. Students who consider themselves slower readers can be very successful on the test, by learning active reading strategies to identify the most important information. Some parts are okay to read less carefully, for example, because they contain details supporting a larger claim or point. Don't add your own soundtrack: The LSAT doesn't require any outside expertise in the many topics it presents to you. All of the information that you need will be presented in the passage. When you bring your own experience, knowledge and opinions about a topic into the mix, you may add your own unwarranted assumptions which will lead you to wrong choices. Strong critical readers avoid this common LSAT pitfall! Don't time yourself too early on: Accuracy, then speed! When learning a new skill, it's better to leave timing considerations to the side until you've increased your skill level enough to warrant timing. If you were learning piano, you wouldn't play a piece at full-speed before you'd practiced the passages very slowly, and then less slowly, and then less slowly still. Do read with your pencil: Reading actively is helpful to understanding reading comprehension passages and not "zoning out" while you read. Many students like to underline or circle keywords, such as "however", "therefore", "argues that", "first/second", and many others that you'll learn throughout your studies with us. If you're reading with your pencil, you're much less likely to wonder what you just read in the last minute, and you can focus on the structure and shifts in the action. Do be nimble: You don't have to do the passages and questions in order, or even to do a given question at all. Many students find success maximizing their score by skipping a select handful of questions entirely, either because they know a question will take too long to solve, or because they just don't know how to solve it. Do learn about all of the question types: An effective approach to a main point question is very different than an effective approach to an inference question, even though the passage is the same. Do spend time on the fundamentals: Effective reading strategies take time to learn and implement consistently. For example, understand how to identify important keywords (and why they're important) before practicing many passages in a row. The hints and explanations in the system will help with this—a lot! Other key skills include characterizing the relationships between various points of view and identifying the purpose of a paragraph. Be patient with yourself! Do honor the precision of language: If the author writes, "This explanation isn't well-supported, however", an inference question might ask you what the author's attitude towards the explanation is. A wrong choice would be something like, "vehement skepticism", whereas the answer might be, "cautious doubt." Many students are too approximate in their reading and it hurts their score on the LSAT; in other words, they see some degree of disagreement and they believe that any choice that expresses disagreement will be correct. They may see the word "most" in the passage and equate it to "all" by mistake.

Writing Sample

The writing prompt presents a situation to you, and you are asked to choose between two positions or courses of action. Both options are defensible, and you are given the parameters and the evidence on which to base your decision. There's no "right" or "wrong" position to take on the subject, so it doesn't matter which side you choose! What is important is how well you support one choice and how well you criticize the other choice.

It's a good idea to read the outline and instructions carefully. Most students find it helpful to spend some time thinking about the subject and organizing their thoughts on paper before they start writing. In your essay, be sure to develop your ideas in full, leaving time, if possible, to review what you've written. Don't write to a topic other than the one you mentioned.

You're not going to need any special knowledge to do well on the writing sample. Law Schools are looking at a number of things: Clarity Organization Language Use Ability to justify a stance Reading logic How well you write is more important than how much you write— many successful students apply only two paragraphs for a sample of reading, with one paragraph reflecting on the option they endorse and another paragraph opposing the other choice. There are many ways to complete a good sample of writing.

Make sure that your writing is readable and that you confine your article to the marked, lined areas on the front and back of the separate Writing Sample Answer Paper, because only that area will be replicated for law schools.

As of June 2019, students do not have to complete a written review immediately after taking the LSAT. Instead, they will complete LSAT Writing (Official New Name) on their own time. Whether it's days, weeks, or even months after the study.

LSAT Writing is a task of 35 minutes. It requires you to write a persuasive essay in favor of a specific choice between two possible options. In the near future, I will discuss the details of the mission, known as the "Decision Prompt." Next, let's discuss some of the important aspects of LSAT Writing itself.

This is important.

Your file is not complete until at least one written sample has been submitted. LSAC is very serious about this! Your Law School Report (compilation of your school records, test scores, sample writing, letter of recommendation, etc.) will not be sent to any law school that you have applied for until it has been completed. You have legally written a sample writing one year from your test date. My recommendation is to get it done sooner rather than later. You don't want to drop the ball and miss the deadline for your application! Keep in mind that LSAC states that it may take 3-4 weeks to process your sample and to update your file.

It just needs to be done once.

Applicants now only need to have a single writing sample on file, even if it's a paper-based test from the past. Re-takers do not have to complete additional LSAT Writing unless they want to do so. You might want to send more than one! Maybe you'd rather have a sample typed in the file than a handwritten essay. If you already have a writing sample in your file and really want to submit another one, you will have to pay a small fee. Schools will receive the 3 most recent samples of writing as part of your Law School Report.

It's unscored.

That's right: your essay isn't going to get a number or a ranking. Unlike the multiple-choice questions you have recently answered on the LSAT, the distinction between "perfect" effort and something unquestionably bad is more qualitative than quantitative. It's primarily a matter of your ability to follow up on a handful of recommendations that I'll describe in depth below.

LSAT Writing is sent to every law school you are applying to. Many are going to skim, and some are going to read it carefully. Don't write it off, then!

The last thing you want is an admissions commitee that reads your essay to think you're not serious about the process. Law School is harsh, It requires a level of herculean dedication. Imagine what a group is telling you to discuss your intentions and potential if you don't commit yourself to half an hour of writing. The risks of dismissal far outweigh the benefits. Plus, according to a few admissions directors I talked to, they're looking at the quality of your unpublished and spontaneous essay as a further indicator of your writing chops. It's at the core of law school success.

You're here to win it, so let's go crazy. I will dissect LSAT Writing piece by piece. From the General Directions to the particular essay Directions to the specifics of the actual proposal. And I'm also going to give you the tools to make an essay that any board would be happy to receive.

General Instructions Per LSAC: "You will have 35 minutes to prepare and write an essay on the subject given [it will be a randomly selected prompt]. Read the subject and instructions carefully. You'll probably find it best to spend a few minutes thinking about the subject and organizing your thoughts before you start writing. In your article, make sure to formulate your ideas in detail, leaving time, if possible, to review what you have learned. Don't write to a topic other than the one you mentioned. Writing on a matter of your own choosing is not appropriate.

For this writing exercise, no special knowledge is required or anticipated. Law Schools are interested in the logic, consistency, structure, language use and writing mechanics shown in your article. How well you write is more important than how much you write. "You'll be able to use scratch paper to sketch any notes or initial thoughts. Use it to jot down pros and cons and build a game plan for your overall response. You'll need to show the camera on both sides of any scratch paper before you start. If you wrap things up early, you'll have time to reread your writing and make quick edits as needed. And, trust me, there's almost certainly going to be a few mistakes to touch up.

Next, this essay is all about your interpretation of the information you're given. It is not about your specific knowledge of the subject or the volume of text you submit. Readers are interested in how persuasive your argument is, and that's it. Reflect on convincingly defending your chosen path and think less about subject knowledge and word count.

Oddly, there's a second set of directions right before the subject of the essay. They are more specific to the nature of the Prompt itself. Before beginning your article, be sure to understand these directions. Reading them again wastes valuable time!

You must make a choice The scenario presented below describes two choices that can be supported on the basis of the information provided. Your essay should consider both choices and argue one over the other on the basis of the criteria and the facts you have provided. There is no "right" or "wrong" choice: a reasonable argument can be made either. Again, easy enough for me. Those instructions detail the key points for what is to come. You have either / or a decision to make with no "right" choice. Information is provided in support of both choices, and yet you have to choose one and stick to it.

This is very critical.

You've got to take a side.

There isn't a clear winner. All options have advantages and disadvantages, but here you can't hedge. You need to choose one and go all-in to defend it. But, as we'll see, that doesn't mean blind devotion. The fact that you lean one way does not mean that the alternative is without merit. Recognizing the occasional failures of your path, while at the same time hinting at the upsides of the other, is what great essays are made of. But in a second, more on that.

Consider this example Let's look at the June 2007 LSAT Writing Sample for a detailed look at exactly how it works. Here's the Writing Review in its entirety from that test.

BLZ Stores, a well-established men's clothing retailer with a chain of stores in the major metropolitan area, is pursuing an expansion plan. Using the facts below, write an essay in which you advocate for one of the following proposals over the other based on the following two criteria: the organization wants to increase profits.

The company is committed to ensuring its long-term financial stability.

The "national plan" is to open a large number of men's clothing stores across the country over a short period of time. In doing so, the company would have incurred considerable debt. It would also have to significantly increase personnel and improve regional marketing and distribution capabilities. Many regional companies that have adopted this strategy have dramatically increased their profits. More tried and failed, with serious financial consequences. Outside its home area, BLZ is not well known. Research indicates that the name of the BLZ is viewed positively by those who know it. National clothing chains can offer lower prices because of their increased purchasing power. BLZ is currently facing ever-increasing competition from such chains in its home region.

The "regional strategy" is to increase the number and size of stores in the home region of the organization and to improve their equipment, merchandise quality and service. This could, for the most part, be done with current cash reserves. Such improvements will usually increase the prices paid by BLZ. For one trial store where such changes were made, sales and profits improved. The local population is on the rise. BLZ enjoys high customer loyalty. Regional expansion could be achieved mainly through the use of seasoned and dedicated BLZ personnel and would allow for continued confidence in well-known and trusted vendors, contractors and other business connections.

As you can see, you have to make one of two choices based on two parameters. In this situation, improved and believed to be somewhat immediate, competitiveness and long-term financial stability. As is the case with every LSAT Writing prompt, the problem is the same. Every option is likely to better fulfill one governing objective while at the same time underperforming the other. In other words, there is no clear winner. An interesting study scenario all about the right answers.

Here, the two options are especially opaque: neither goal seems to be explicitly accomplished. Still, you can expect to assign each option to an objective, which provides a starting point. What are My goals, and which strategy is best suited to each?

Through earnings, which means that I need a way to generate revenue and ideally as quickly as possible. Although the "national plan" relates to gain, it is also an expensive and seemingly high-risk step in the short term. From a profit perspective, it seems more appropriate to follow a "regional strategy" in which BLZ avoids serious debt by using its cash reserves to increase the size and number of its stores and rapidly raise prices.

Essentially, this option requires little change in infrastructure. As a result, it makes for some potentially fast tests, as previously observed in the trial shop. Nevertheless, it does not offer much in the way of long-term growth / stability. It only refers to stores in the home region of the business where I are advised that pressure is growing. In a way, this is a much more gradual, small-scale improvement than the alternative. But with the potential to generate small yet rapid financial gains.

Ensure long-term financial stability, which means that I need a way to protect ourselves against future losses over the years, maybe decades. With the talk of increasing competition in the home region of BLZ, the "national plan" seems to provide a more enticing long-term, large-scale solution. There are, of course, greater risks than with the national strategy. BLZ must incur significant debt, commit significant resources to new staff and marketing / distribution activities. I will also face an uphill battle with not-so-great odds, given the historical implications for other businesses that have implemented this approach. But with a strong reputation and a need to grow beyond their home region, the long-term survival of the business may well rely on this broad-based approach.

There are two things about these bullets. Next, I tried to categorize the two proposals according to their probability of meeting the criteria set out. Usually, it's a lot more black and white to see which plan serves which goal. This specific study is embarrassingly vague. I also explained my rationale as to why I combined them as I did and listed the downsides of each of them. That's basically how you're supposed to begin the planning phase of your essay. Consider how to combine a choice with the criteria that best meets and why. At the same time, assess the forms in which it falls short of perfection. Second, I wouldn't write that out on the real thing, at least not like I did here. I just listed it to show the process of thinking behind the assignments I've chosen.

Alternatively, what I recommend you do to keep this method structured is to build an x-, y-axis style graph on your scratch paper. Here you can list the Pros and Cons of each option so that you don't forget any of them when you start to write.

Now you can quickly categorize the advantages and disadvantages of the two plans according to the requirements on offer. So if I were to fill in each of those quadrants, it would seem like... At this stage, the only thing left to do before I get to write is to pick a side. Again, there is no right or wrong answer. Choose which choice you believe you're better able to defend based on the points you've just outlined. Anything appears to appeal to you or that you believe has more appealing pros and/or less negative cons.

For me, with this specific idea, I would have preferred a regional strategy. Here's the reason. The regional strategy tends to provide greater immediate opportunities for low-risk financial success. While it is unlikely to be a permanent solution to the company's long-term goals if it produces quick profits with little investment. It would, in turn, minimize the consequences of eventually pursuing a more nationally-oriented expansion. In short, use the regional strategy now, make as much money as possible from your loyal local customer base before the market becomes unsustainable. Then use those benefits to cover the "significant debt" associated with something more ambitious down the road.

Note that I'm not recommending to do both of them!"That would have been a mistake. I have taken a vote in favor of one over the other. Nonetheless, my logic may still allow for the possibility that doing one now does not necessarily prevent the potential existence of the other at some point in the future. In this scenario, unless, of course, the initial option is entirely based on the product, there is a very real concern with the national plan.

Let's Recap: You have to make a decision between competing choices with no right or wrong answer and opposing points for and against each choice based on a pair of desired outcomes. You must choose, despite not being the perfect solution, spend a few minutes deciding which option is best suited to the parameters given, and make a quick sketch to mention the pros and cons of each choice. Once you choose a strategy that you are more equipped to defend, you defend it while considering the downsides of your decision and the possible upsides of the alternative.

For a lot of students out there, the most common essay form is the classic, high school-favorite five paragraph answer. This is far too much involved in this mission. Alternatively, I encourage you to make the following quick, two-paragraph essay.

Paragraph 1: Your choice : Begin with a clear statement indicating which of the two options you have chosen. So spend the rest of the first paragraph on the defense of that decision: explain why your pros are important and appropriate, and the motivating forces behind the choice, and downplay the flaws that your selection includes. This is very significant! You need to explicitly mention that your option is actually a mistake, at which point you can then explain why their consequences are not a deal-breaker.

One of the primary concerns of anyone reading your article is whether you were honest and rational in your handling of an incomplete proposal. Note, recognizing a degree of weakness can actually be an asset,if you approach it proactively and minimize its nastier effects. This is your chance to do just that.

Paragraph 2: Alternative: In your second paragraph, you will provide a justification for rejecting the other alternative, in particular by the its advantages and emphasizing its shortcomings.

Again, you need to admit that this choice has some merit. Doing so shows that you're not just fair— a sort of diplomacy goes a long way here — but it also helps youto de-emphasize certain advantages.

Finally, end this article with a sentence that easily reaffirms your decision and, in broad terms, how the knowledge you have received speaks in favor of it.

Of course, if you have a few minutes left — and it's a good idea to pace yourself so that you do — read what you've written and look for typos, mispellings, and grammatical errors that the word processing functions might overlook. Those issues won't keep you out of law school if you're otherwise eligible, but they don't make a great impression. Clean it up if you can do that.

In Summary

I've given more of a guide for how to compose an essay than an "ideal" sample essay itself.

While I strongly encourage you to adhere to the points and patterns outlined above, the reason for this is that I am not here to dictate your writing style. Your voice is yours, and it's crucial that it rings true and reads authentically in your essay.

Are there simple rules that you should follow? Yeah, yeah. And the text here is supposed to give you a clear idea of what these are. But it's up to you to fill the gaps with the words—

and the reasoning — of your creation. Luckily, by following this guide, I'm confident that you won't have any trouble expressing yourself commendably when it counts.

Example Directions: The scenario presented below identifies two options, each of which can be supported on the basis of the information provided. Your essay will consider both options and argue for one over the other on the basis of the two requirements and the evidence presented. There is no "right" or "wrong" choice: a fair argument can be made either.

Change the specifics Prompt: Two pediatricians determine whether to move their small practice 10 miles away, to a large medical pavilion downtown, or to maintain their current location, and also to open a second office about 20 miles across the area. Using the facts below, write an essay in which you argue for one choice over the other on the basis of the following two criteria: physicians want to attract new patients.

The doctors are trying to keep their current customers.

The Laurel Medical Pavilion is a new collection of medical office buildings next to the city's main hospital. The pavilion is suitable for public transport. It offers plenty of free parking space. Although the office space in the pavilion is costly, it's going fast. The space that the pediatricians would lease includes five examination rooms, ample office space, and a large waiting area that the doctors would be able to furnish as they like. The pavilion rents rooms to doctors in a wide range of fields. This provides equipment for a wide range of clinical and diagnostic tests.

The building that doctors consider leasing as a second office is, like their current premises, a 100-year-old Victorian house in a predominantly residential area full of young families. The house has a wide fenced-in and off-street parking area for five vehicles. The first floor of the building has recently been remodeled to meet the needs of a small medical practice. As their present premises, it comprises three consultation rooms, a small waiting room and adequate office space. The second floor has not been transformed into an acceptable working area. The doctors have the option of doing so.

How could I get started?

Thirty-five minutes is typically more than enough time for you to apply a high-quality sample of writing, given that you schedule your writing accordingly.Isuggest that you spend about 10-15 minutes preparing before you start writing.

- List your choices.
- Relocation 10 miles away (large medical pavilion downtown) Keep your office in place and open your second office for about 20 miles across the area.
- List the conditions for this.
- Attract new patients, keep current patients on the list.
- List 2-3 pros and cons of each decision.

Most students find it helpful to hang on to decision making until they have established the benefits and drawbacks of each decision, as it often becomes apparent in this process which decision will be easier to defend. Note, there is no "right" or "wrong" decision, but you will usually feel at least slightly more comfortable defending one than the other.

Relocate about 10 mi. Downtown (large med. pavilion) Convenient for public transport. (Good for attracting new patients) 10 miles a

way (harder to keep current patients) Convenient to access other health services (good for attracting new patients + keeping up-to-date) Expensive (potentially less money for building clientele through marketing, technology, etc.) Keep up-to-date office and open second office Less chance of losing current patients as they can continue to goto pre-study.

Now make a decision that made it easier for you to justify while you were brainstorming. We're going to take the decision to keep this office and open an additional office 20 miles away. It's important to be concise and decisive for your writing sample— law schools are concerned about the quality of your writing and rhetoric, not the length of time alone.

Organize your question.

One simple structure for a written sample is to make a decision in the first paragraph and defend it, and then address one potential strength of the decision that you have rejected. In the second paragraph, you can then discuss why you rejected the other decision, while also recognizing the weakness of the decision that you supported. That may sound somewhat abstract, so here's a possible outline: paragraph 1: Keep the office in place and open the second office.

Less chance of losing current patients as they can continue to go to the current office Largely residential area full of young families (good for attracting new patients because they are pediatricians)* Two offices should attract more new patients than one office would One weakness of the chosen decision: it is true that the space that pediatricians consider for their second office is less spacious.

Paragraph 2: Don't move anywhere.

One strength of the rejected decision:* While the downtown office does have immediate proximity to health services such as hospitals and diagnostic tests, it comes with the steep literal cost of renting office space, and the steep figurative price of losing existing clientele who do not want to drive 10 miles downtown.

The doctors would miss out on the thriving market of the young families the second office would represent.

Write down the sample.

The toughest and most critical work needs to be done! Now, use descriptive writing and correct terminology, making a good transition from idea to idea ("first," "second," "finally," for example), and keeping the doctor's guidelines as consistent as possible, you should be able to write a very powerful essay.

A few final thoughts on Spelling's writing sample problems. If you're not sure how to spell it, it's better to use another term that you know how to spell.

Choose a side of it and stick with it. Be sure about your decision— don't ride the fence and seek to make a strong case for both decisions.

Write it simply. Practice writing legibly in your pencil if you don't feel confident about your ability to do so.

Don't get carried away. This isn't a "law school essay." Everything you need to use is in the writing prompt, so you shouldn't be pulling in any outside knowledge beyond what's common knowledge.

Logical reasoning

Every Logical Reasoning question requires you to read and understand a short passage, and then answer a question about it. The questions are structured to test a wide range of critical thinking skills.

The Logical Reasoning (LR) section of the LSAT consists of two 35-minute exams with approximately 25 questions each. It is part of the LSAT that most specifically tests the abilities that you will use as a lawyer— understanding and evaluating the case and finding holes in it, or, if it is true, taking the argument to its logical conclusion. When it comes to your LSAT score, Logical Reasoning is twice as important as any other portion of the test due to the fact that the LSAT includes two LR sections, as opposed to just one 35-minute Reading Comprehension or Analytical Reasoning. And, even if you shine on the other pages, you can't get a high score on the LSAT without doing well in the Logical Reasoning.

Because of its importance and complexity, I'm goingto spend a lot of time discussing the Logical Reasoning study tips. I will break down basic concepts, problem forms, underlying assumptions, problems, types of arguments and argumentation patterns, what separates a weak argument from a strong argument, and more, show you how to logically differentiate the argument piece by piece in order to determine the correct answer.

Hold the following general knowledge in mind throughout the Logical Reasoning section: The score depends on the number of correct answers— not the number of wrong answers— so you are not penalized for guessing.

You are not trying to determine whether the argument itself is correct, but whether it is logical or not. It means that sometimes the right answer to a question will contain a statement or knowledge that is not valid in the true word. As counter-intuitive as it may seem, understanding the relationship between the different facts and the assumptions that lead to that answer is more important than the objective accuracy of the choice of an argument or answer. Answer using the information provided in the question only. The opposite is true, too–sometimes an incorrect choice of answer will contain information that is true in the real world.

Assuming that you have studied the different types of arguments used in the Logical Reasoning section, the best approach is to start by determining which type of question you are looking at. Precisely defining the type of question will be a great help in separating the correct answers from the wrong ones.

How to Answer Logical Reasoning Questions Identifying the type of question is essential when determining how to approach the Logical Reasoning Question. Here are the Most Common Logical Reasoning Question Types: Flaw Questions ask you to find the underlying flaw in the argument put forward.

Assumption Questions ask you to describe the difference between the facts and the inference reached. The right choice of answer will be the argument that is appropriate to get from the proof to the conclusion.

Inference Questions ask to find the statement most supported by the argument, assuming that all the statements in the argument are true.

Strengthen Questions asks you to consider a sentence that would better illustrate the author's argument and endorse the inference.

Weaken Questions ask you to see an argument that would most contradict the author's evidence in support of the claim.

Paradox Questions ask you to remember the choice of answer with the same statement form as the one in the question.

Theory Questions ask you to choose a choice of answer that is an example of the concept or theory stated in the statement.

Anyway, take a deep breath— you're probably looking at one of those kinds of questions.

Your approach will, of course, vary depending on the type of question you answer. You don't want to choose a choice of answer that strengthens the argument when the question asks which option will help weaken the claim!

So, be sure to get acquainted with the most common logical reasoning questions. You want to know all the forms of the Logical Reasoning problem so well that on the day of the LSAT, you will feel confident and know exactly what to do. No hesitation from you— you'll be ready to crush any question that the test throws in your way!

Then do as much practice as you can!

Read the argument carefully.

Read Actively

Just like when you read a paragraph in the Reading Comprehension section, you're going to want to read Logical Reasoning points actively, make notes, and share keywords and phrases. This isn't easy to read — dissect the logic and grasp how all the sentences fit together.

Define the conclusion & premise In order to answer the logical reasoning question correctly, you must correctly identify the conclusion of the statement and the premise or the supporting sentence. Remember that the conclusion is not always at the end of the argument (though that would be nice!). Be on the lookout for keywords that signal the conclusion; words like "hence" or "henceforth" generally signal the end. Helpful tip:

watch these helpful terms throughout the LSAT for both the Logical Reasoning and Reading Comprehension parts!

Circle Important Keywords When you read the argument, you'll want to be on the lookout for other keywords. Some of the key words on the LSAT include "except," "some," and "few." Always circle those words when you see them— it's almost certain they're going to be important when you find the right answer. (And don't forget these words once you're in your dream law school— the legal interpretations turn on them, too!) Quick review of the type of question!

Just before you evaluate the choice of answer, do a quick review of the type of question. After two hours of testing, it's easy to get tired and forget what the question asked you to do.

So, always do a quick review of the type of question. With a clear sense of what the problem is, you're going to be able to find the right answer and pick up another point!

Analyze the choice of answer.

Identifying the right choice of answer to the Logical Reasoning problem is a comparative method. There could be two really good answers. Your mission, if you choose to accept it, is to find the best one. While that might sound tricky, there are a few approaches to find the right one.

Next, don't be led astray by any wrong choices of response. Delete any obvious, wrong choices easily. This will help narrow the scope of the remaining responses. Through going through the obvious wrong responses, you have already improved the chances of getting the right answer.

Second, read each of the remaining responses as carefully as you read the statement. One word can alter the whole context of the answer, and it costs you a point in the process — don't let it happen to you! Read each choice of answer carefully to make sure you answer the exact question you were asked to answer.

If the answer to the question is an option, don't stop there. You've got to read all the other choices to make sure you've found the best answer to your choice. Note, there are likely to be two good choices.

Keep moving, don't get bogged down on a single question. Keep in mind that every question on the LSAT is worth the same as every other question. If you really find yourself stuck on a question, use the elimination process to at least narrow your choice of answer.

Then, choose what you think is the best answer from the remaining choices and move on! Next to the question in your test booklet, you can draw a big star and come back if you have time left at the end of the segment.

Practice this in your timed practice sections. You want the process of moving on when you're stuck to be second nature on LSAT Day. Always be ready to get to your next point!

And remember: speed is important. You only have 35 minutes to answer 25 Logical Reasoning questions.

If Logical Reasoning is your most or least favorite part of the LSAT, you have to prepare to do well on this half of the exam and to excel on the LSAT.

Hold the five tips in mind while you're practicing: read the question first, and define the type of question.

Common Logical Reasoning Questions on the LSAT

You're going to come across all kinds of arguments on the test. The argument may be logically faulty, or it may be perfectly logical. It could be weak or strong. Your role in this section of the LSAT will be to understand the argument quickly and precisely, and then to evaluate it in some way on the basis of the requirements in question. In some cases, you're not going to have a lot of trouble doing that, but for most of the questions, you're going to have to do some serious thinking to get the right answer.

If the stimulus includes an argument, no matter what kind of argument it is, it will consist of two basic elements–thepremise(s) and the conclusion. The argument is the point that the author is trying to persuade the reader of, while the hypotheses are the facts that he presents to support his claim. In other words, the inference of the author is the content of his case, and the premises are the explanation for it. Here's an example of a simple, succinct argument: Argument example, Alice has a 4.0 GPA, and she scored a 99th percentile on the Medical College Admission Test, so she's sure to be accepted to elite medical school.

The implication is that Alice should not think about being admitted by the prestigious medical school. It is believed that she has a 4.0 GPA and that her MCAT score is 99th percentile. So, asIhave said, this is a very basic argument, so let's add some additional information: Alice has a 4.0 GPA, and she scored a 99th percentile on the Medical College Admission Test, so she's sure to be admitted to the prestigious medical school. She will be at the top of her class with her work and study habits. Once she graduates, due to her prestigious degree and background, she will have her choice of residences. Obviously, Alice is going to have a very successful career in medicine.

This shifts things a little bit. The new argument, although not very complex, is certainly more complicated than the one in the first paragraph. Note that the point the author was trying to make in the first passage is no longer his conclusion. His latest assumption is that Alice is going to have a very good career in medicine. What's wrong with his previous conclusion? It has now become a sub-conclusion that helps to build up the case for his actual conclusion. You're going to run into this kind of argument on the LSAT several times. It's important to be able to discern a sub-conclusion from a conclusion, so you need to read it carefully. Additionally, there is no logic rule that says the inference will come at the end of the statement. Look at how I can rearrange this argument: Alice is going to have a very good career in medicine. She has a 4.0 GPA and scored in the 99th percentile on the Medical College Admission Test, so she's sure to be admitted to the elite medical school. She will be at the top of her class with her work and study habits. Once she graduates, due to her prestigious degree and background, she will have her choice of residences.

It makes the same point as before, but it's worded differently. The conclusion is now in the first sentence, which appears before the sub-conclusion. And keep in mind that the inference will appear anywhere in the statement. In fact, there may also be more than one sub-conclusion. Careful reading is as important to the Logical Reasoning part of the LSAT as it is to the other parts.

Do NOT Read the Question First

You need to decide on a consistent strategy to attack each Logical Reasoning issue long before you get to the testing center. In fact, you're supposed to do this before you even start taking practice tests. So, what's the best strategy for that? My strong recommendation is that you should always read the statement before you read the question. It is important to note that this is the same approach that I suggest you use in the Reading Comprehension portion of the LSAT. In fact, I suggest that one of the worst things you can do in the Reading Comprehension segment is to read the questions first and second, even though this is a popular strategy. The same applies to the Logical Reasoning portion of the LSAT. Reading the question first will often cause you to be distracted or confused while reading the argument, and in almost all cases you will end up having to read the question again anyway, wasting a lot of valuable time. Don't try to read the issue first, then the point. You're just going to slow down, making it even harder to answer all the questions in a very fast thirty-five minutes.

Opposites Sometimes, when two responses are a pair of direct opposites, one of them is right. The paragraph or sentence will often include established relationships (e.g. when this goes up, it goes down). The question can ask you to draw conclusions from this and offer two similar answers to the choices that are opposed to each other.

Example: 1) If other factors are kept constant, then an increase in the interest rate will lead to a decrease in housing starts 2) If other factors are kept constant, then an increase in the interest rate will lead to an increase in housing starts Once you know that there are two alternative options, you will analyze them closely. One of them is likely to be the correct answer. Of course, they're often not as easy to spot as the two answers in this example. In many cases, the wording of the two choices will not be nearly as similar to each other as the above. However, it is the meanings that are important, not the specific phrase.

Watch Out for Red Herings: It's a literary device used by authors to mislead people to draw a wrong conclusion about something or someone in the plot. This system is often used by novelists and scriptwriters. For example, in a murder mystery, the butler of a dead man may be implicitly depicted as scheming and selfish, leading many readers to believe that he committed the murder. At the end of the day, however, the grieving widow is revealed to be the real culprit, notwithstanding the putative greed and deceit of the butler.

Well, novelists and scriptwriters are not the only people who regularly use red herrings in their line of work; so are the people in the Law School Admission Council, who are responsible for creating the LSAT. In fact, creating red herrings is a huge part of their work. The designers of the exam intentionally make the wrong answer choices that are very close to correct. One of the most important tasks of their job is to go to great lengths to try to convince you to choose the wrong answer, and, apparently, they wouldn't be very successful if none of the wrong answers were plausible. If that were the case, all you would have to do would be to go down the list and eliminate the four choices that are clearly inescapable, and the only one left would be the correct answer. That kind of exam wouldn't be a big challenge, obviously.

Though, there will be three answers to most of the Logical Reasoning questions that aren't all that close to being correct, and only one that could really trip you up. That's because there's just not a lot of ways to come up with an answer choice that sounds almost right, but it's not. An answer that is almost right but that doesn't have to strike the test taker as incredibly probable, and that makes it very difficult to produce the wrong answers that seem to be accurate. And, for the most part, you shouldn't have the trouble to sort out the blatantly incorrect responses.

Once you've eliminated the obvious wrong answers, you just have to choose between two options. This is the good news. The bad news is that while removing three answer options that make it a bit easier to choose the correct answer, it certainly doesn't make it a snap, because now you're going to have to determine which of the remaining two responses is correct, and which one is an artfully crafted red herring.

There are a number of kinds of red herrings. Here are some that LSAT designers employ most of the time.

1. Taking Things to the Extreme In many cases, the LSAT writers will include a choice of response that takes the point made in the passage to an unjustified edge. Remember this passage: many so-called conservatives are willing to see America go to war, while at the same time condemning President Jones for running massive federal deficits. This doesn't make any sense. One of the fundamental basic principles of populism is the government's aversion to deficit spending. Okay, President Jones is not to blame for these huge budget deficits; they are actually the fault of his ostensibly conservative predecessor, President Smith, who quickly initiated a long and costly war without considering all other options.

In view of the above argument, which of the following must be true?

The speaker of the passage is a Liberal President Smith was a Republican People who are true conservatives should not be willing to go to war, as wars contribute to budget deficits.

Most conservatives think that going to war is more important than having a balanced budget.

AsImentioned earlier, on most of the cases, you can expect to find three responses that you can easily dismiss. Let's look at every comment, starting with A. If the argument is correct, is it also true that President Jones is not a conservative? Yeah, no, not at all.Iknow that many professing conservatives are condemning Jones to large deficits, but that doesn't mean that Jones is a liberal or a moderate. Most political activists are more strident about condemning politicians of their own beliefs who struggle to please them than they are about condemning politicians in other camps. Thus, there is absolutely nothing in the passage that means that it must be true that President Jones is not a conservative. A is gone, therefore.

So how about B, is it necessarily true that the speaker of the passage is a liberal? Once, the answer to that is no. There is nothing in the passage that allows us to believe that the speaker is a liberal. He might well be, but he might also be a disappointed republican. For that matter, he could be a centrist, or even an apolitical guy, and that claim could be part of a larger "pox on both houses" story. So it's easy to dismiss B.

Moving to C, does it logically follow from the passage that the former president was a Republican? No, it's not. Now, of the three answers that are obviously wrong, this is the one that would most likely travel a few people up because of careless reading and mentally bringing facts to the real world to solve the problem. I learn from the passage that President Smith is said to have been independent. However, I don't know anything about his party affiliation. While most people rightly equate the conservative label with the Republican Party in the real world of American politics, that doesn't mean that there aren't some Democrats who call themselves conservatives. In fact, in the 1992 election, Bill Clinton and Al Gore won by selling themselves as conservative democrats, in contrast to liberals like Michael Dukakis and Walter Mondale. But conservative doesn't have to say Conservative. In fact, the passage does not address Republicans or Democrats at all. It could be defined as a hypothetical future America in which neither party exists any longer. But C is incorrect, too, and that's pretty obvious.

So we've got two answers left to choose from. Is D the right choice for you? May I infer from the passage that conflicts are contributing to budget deficits? A lot of people would choose this answer. Could you please? You're not meant to, as the logic is flawed. In fact, it's a great example of how LSAT designers are driving people up. Let's take a closer look at it.

In this red herring, the test designers take a specific point, but then make too much of it. They begin with an indisputable fact from the passage–the author said that President Jones should not be blamed for the huge federal budget deficits he had suffered during his tenure; the blame should actually be given to the man he had succeeded, President Smith, who had waged an expensive war while he was in the White House. This is a perfectly reasonable argument, because wars are usually very expensive, and in America's recent history, they have definitely led to massive deficit spending. Also, for the purposes of the LSAT, I should assume that the facts presented in the argument are true, unless otherwise stated.

However, most republicans support fiscal restraint and are generally opposed to running up deficits. So, a very good case can be made that people who are true conservatives should have opposed President Smith's putting America in a costly war before all other options had failed. However, the answer to choice D goes much further than that. It says that wars are leading to budget deficits. It doesn't mean that wars tend to lead to budget deficits, or that most wars in history have contributed to deficit spending. This makes a categorical statement that war results in budget deficits. This is a statement if / then. Remember, if / then statements rarely appear in their pure form on the Logical Reasoning exam. They're usually implied. In this sentence, the expression, since wars lead to budget deficits, contains the following if / then statement: if a country goes to war, it will experience budget deficits.

However, this is not logically the result of the information I have in the passage. There is nothing in the passage that tells us that all wars in history have caused budget deficits, or that all wars in the future will do so, let alone that war always leads to budget deficits. What I learn from the passage is that the huge federal deficits under President Jones preceded the war that President Smith had ended. Does this mean that all battles, all over the world, all the time, lead to budget deficits? Is it possible to imagine a situation in which a nation goes to war and does not suffer budget deficits as a result?

Isn't it possible for a country's government to fund a war without running up deficits by using budget surpluses left over from previous years, or raising taxes, or a combination of both? Yeah, well, it could. Isn't it also possible that if Nation A goes to war with Nation B, Nation B could surrender almost immediately, resulting in a very short and very cheap war, the cost of which could be entirely covered by Nation A's current military budget? Yes, this is certainly a possibility, too.

Therefore, based on the information in the passage, I can not categorically say that wars contribute to budget deficits. The fact that President Smith's wars resulted in budget deficits does not mean that all wars must have the same impact. D is therefore wrong, even though it seems to make sense. It's wrong because it's going to the extreme, taking one instance of something and making it a strict, quick statute.

Note that this tactic of going to extremes is also working in the opposite direction. Instead of making a leap from something that happens in one case to a rule that happens in each case, the choice of answer could just as easily lead to an illogical conclusion that, because something did not happen in a specific case, it never happens in any case.

Watch carefully for categorical words in arguments and answer choices, such as always, all, must, never, none, can't, only, absolutely, certainly, and so on. If one of these terms appears in the choice of answer, it is usually incorrect, unless the statement also makes a similar categorical assertion, either expressed or implied. If one of these kinds of terms occurs in the statement itself, then search for an answer option that suits it.

Keep in mind, however, that there can be a categorical statement without using any of these typeff words. In the example above, the word "everything" does not appear in the crucial phrase because wars lead to budget deficits. It is clearly implied, however, that there are no such changes as some or most in the phrase that would restrict the argument as referring only to a number of wars less than all.

E is the correct answer. Note that the term "many" is used as an editor, just as the author does, and does not make a general assertion about all the conservatives. WhenIconclude that the argument is valid, this implies that the first sentence of the argument must be true, which logically leads to the assumption contained in E.

Irrelevance Similar Language Parallel Reasoning You're going to run across a variety of responses that seem to be correct, but are actually completely irrelevant to the argument. You will also find answers that try to trip you up using a language that is similar to some of the language used in the passage.

You will also come across incorrect answers that seem right because they use parallel logic.

Sometimes you will encounter answers that combine two or more red herrings. Here's an example of a mixture of Irrelevance, Common Words, and Parallel Reasoning.

Let's go back to the same point, but change things a little at the end: many so-called conservatives seem willing to have America go to war, while at the same time criticizing President Jones for running up massive federal deficits. This doesn't make any sense. One of the fundamental basic principles of populism is the government's aversion to deficit spending. Okay, President Jones is not to blame for these huge budget deficits; they are actually the fault of his ostensibly conservative predecessor, President Smith, who quickly initiated a long and costly war without considering all other options. So-called conservatives who support rushing to war are not real conservatives.

Now, suppose the question was: which of the following, if true, would reinforce the argument the most?

And suppose this was one of the answer choices: historically, conservatives have strongly condemned homosexuality, but today many so-called conservatives are actually advocating the legalization of same-sex marriages.

Would this statement reinforce the argument? It might seem at first glance. The fact that people who favor same-sex marriage would not have been seen as liberals in past generations appears to go along with what the author says. Did he not mention that many self-proclaimed conservatives have moved away from their fundamental principles? When conservatives used to strongly oppose homosexuality, but many conservatives today approve of same-sex marriage, isn't that proof that many of today's self-proclaimed conservatives aren't true conservatives that supports the author's argument? A lot of people would have preferred this answer option.

Nevertheless, the author's argument is not that many self-proclaimed conservatives are not true conservatives because they have moved away from some basic principles. He only mentions one fundamental principle of conservatism–opposition to deficit spending, and that is the only standard he uses to determine whether someone is a true conservative.

Here is his argument in the form of syllogism: the recent war has led to budget deficits. True conservatives are opposed to budget deficits. Anyone who is eager to go to war is not a real conservative.

The author's argument is very narrowly focused and does not discuss any other element of conservatism other than resistance to deficit spending.Ihave no idea whether he thinks that self-described conservatives have moved away from any other basic principles of conservatism, or whether he even maintains that opposition to homosexuality is a fundamental principle of conservatism. So this choice of answer does not reinforce the author's argument at all. What conservatives now believe, or used to believe, about homosexuality or same-sex marriage has absolutely no bearing on the author's argument that anyone eager to go to war is not a true conservative. Not only does this choice of answer fail to validate the point, it is completely irrelevant. It would, however, fool a lot of test takers.

Why is this choice of response so misleading? Why is it that many people think it reinforces the author's argument when it's completely irrelevant in actuality? There are several reasons why this answer would fool a lot of test-takers. First of all, it is factually true–almost all the liberals of past generations have treated homosexuality as highly immoral, but these days many have opposed and even approved same-sex marriages. This is enough on its own to trick many of the reviewers into choosing this answer.

I can't stress enough that you don't have to take real-world factual accuracy into account at all in this portion of the LSAT; you have to think of yourself as being in a self-contained universe when answering questions in the Logical Reasoning segment of the test. Ignore everything outside the universe, because the only things that matter are those you're working with on the exam, and some of them would be incorrect in the real world. You must be constantly on guard against this tendency to work with factual accuracy in the response selection process, because it is very easy to fall into it without even realizing it.

Another reason why the choice of answer is so misleading is that it uses some of the same language that the author uses when he mentions self-proclaimed conservatives. This is the very same expression used by the author of the paragraph in the first section. Most test-takers would not even notice this, but their brains would nevertheless make a connection between this response and the statement without knowing it, simply because they use the same word.

In fact, the term is pejorative, as the so-called phrase is used only to describe someone whomIdo not find to be genuine, as a real deal. No one would use the word "expert" to describe someone they find to be a true expert. By using this particular phrase, both the passage and the answer option express the impression that there are a lot of false conservatives out there. BecauseMyminds are looking for reasons to make connections, and because there is often more than one connection, it is easy to mistakenly conclude that since the choice of answer supports the author's view that many people who call themselves conservatives are not such a thing, it also supports his main argument. (Once again, this would not actually be a conscious process of thinking.) At the end of the day, the wrong answer uses parallel logic. Both the response and the passage say that many people who consider themselves conservatives are not real conservatives, and they both do so on the basis of what the writer sees as a failure or inability on the part of these people to measure up to a certain level, not taking the stance that all (or almost all) conservatives used to take. SinceMybrain is constantly looking for patterns and correlations, and because these two statements are so close in their reasoning, many people would assume that the choice of answer strongly supports the statement, but that's not true. It is a similar argument in its form, but it does nothing to support the author's point.

Benchmark After you read the first choice of answer, decide whether or not it sounds correct. If it doesn't, move to the next choice of answer. If you do, make a mental note of it. This doesn't mean you've certainly selected it as your choice of answer; it just means that it's the best you've seen so far. Go ahead and read your next choice. If the next choice is worse than the one you've already chosen, go to the next answer option. If the next choice is better than the one you have already selected, give it your preliminary answer. Repeat this process until all five answer choices have been made.

The first choice of answer that you choose will become your standard. Any other choice of answer must be benchmarked against that norm. The choice is correct until it has been proved otherwise by another choice of answer to beat it out. Once you have decided that no other choice of answer appears to be as good, do a final check to ensure that it answers the question you have asked.

New Information: Right responses will usually contain only the information in the article and/or question. It is rarely possible to insert completely new information into the correct answer choice. Occasionally, new information may be linked in a way that LSAT requires you to understand, but this is uncommon.

Example: The above argument depends on which of the following assumptions?

A. Researchers have used the rule of Charles to explain the relationship.

If the law of Charles is not stated at all in the paragraph and statement referred to above, it is very doubtful that this option is right. All the information you need to answer the question is given to you, so you should not have to make guesses that are unsupported or choose responses that apply to unknown details that can not be analyzed.

Not all claims in the Logical Reasoning Test will include if / then clauses. In many cases, you will need to judge the argument on the basis of how fair it is. That is, you're going to have to ask yourself if the inference makes sense on the basis of the evidence presented. Or is the author making an unfounded claim because he did not provide sufficient evidence to support his conclusion? This is a lot of what you're going to do on the Logical Reasoning portion of the LSAT.

This is, of course, what the jury does in criminal trials. The prosecutor makes a case against the defendant, and the jury weighs the evidence that he presents. When they conclude that the evidence is strong enough that there can be no reasonable doubt that the defendant has committed the crime, they will find him guilty. In most civil trials, though, the burden of proof is not as high–there only has to be a preponderance of evidence for order to assign responsibility. In other words, the complainant only has to present evidence in a civil trial that shows that it is more likely than not that the other person has committed the crime of which he is accused.

At the other end of the scale, Iall come across people making completely unwarranted leaps of logic on a regular basis, particularly while we're surfing the internet or watching cable news talk shows. In those settings, it's common to see people making outlandish claims based on very little or no evidence at all: the federal government's response to Hurricane Katrina proves that George Bush is a racist who hates black people.

Anyone who opposes raising the minimum wage is a Marxist who wants to destroy the American way of life.

Of course, most of the argumentsIencounter on a daily basis fall somewhere in the middle of the two extremes, beyond a reasonable doubt, and completely nonsensical.

Consider this: Jenny said that the new Italian café was fantastic. We're supposed to go there for lunch tomorrow.

A lot of people wouldn't find that to be a point, but it is. Your friend has come to a conclusion (we should have lunch at the new restaurant tomorrow) and is trying to convince you that his conclusion is correct by presenting the evidence on which he is based (Jenny has raved about the place). Is that a reasonable argument? This depends on a lot of different factors. How long have you been friends with Jenny? Do you trust her judgment when it comes to food and dining? How much do you know about Italian food? Was her cousin the director of an Italian café? Is the speaker telling the truth about what Jenny was saying?

If you trust the person who told you this, and you think that Jenny has a good track record when it comes to restaurant recommendations, that argument would probably seem quite reasonable to you. The fact that Jenny was vowing for the place would be enough evidence for you to agree with your friend's conclusion that you should have lunch there tomorrow.

So, consider this argument: Jenny knows good food, so she loves a Mexican restaurant on 23rd street that's on sale. We're supposed to buy it and rent it.

Is that a reasonable argument? In other words, did your friend provide enough evidence to support his conclusion? Even if Jenny is a little bit of a connoisseur, is the fact that she likes food in a restaurant enough evidence to agree that putting tens of thousands of dollars (or more) into an extremely risky business venture is a good idea? No, not really, really. Now, the premise behind the claim is not entirely illogical–after all, people generally buy or start a business in hopes of making a lot of money, popular restaurants strive to make a lot of money, good food is one of the key factors that make restaurants successful, and

Jenny, who is a very good food judge, says the restaurant's food is very good. Therefore, there may be some legitimate reasons to consider the idea of buying a restaurant.

However, there are many other factors that need to be considered before making such a decision that your friend has not even mentioned. Why is that for sale? What do you and your buddy know about the restaurant? How much is the price you asked for? Even if you have agreed that buying a restaurant is a good idea, do you really want to be part of a business partnership? If that is the case, will your friend make a good business partner? These are just a few of the dozens of questions you'd need to answer before you agree to buy a restaurant with your mate. So, while there may be a good idea at its root, the argument is not reasonable, because your friend has not provided nearly enough evidence to support it.

Cause and effect should help you to determine the relative strength or weakness of a particular argument. Since it is possible that A caused B, you will then have to determine whether it is likely that A caused B or whether there are other causative agents that are more likely to have caused B. For instance:

It didn't seem that the store that burned down was doing well. I'm sure it was torched by the owner for the insurance money. Is this a reasonable conclusion as to what caused the fire that burned down the store? No, it's not really. It's a very long logical leap to say that because the store that burned down didn't seem to be doing well, the owner probably set fire to it. As one thing, how do I know what kind of financial condition the store had in it? Let's say I came to the conclusion that the store was failing because I never saw customers coming in or out.

Okay, there might be a lot of reasons for that. Perhaps the only time I went through the store was on my way to and from work every weekday, and the store's top sales were at night and on weekends. It is also quite possible that, like many brick and mortar companies these days, the store made far more money from selling goods over the internet than it did from walking-in traffic, but still had enough local customers to make it profitable to keep the doors open.

It's also quite plausible that the company was only a little profitable, but for whatever reason the owner didn't have to make a lot of money for the shop, and he was quite satisfied with the profits he brought in. There are a lot of reasons why My notion that the store was in bad financial shape might be wrong. However, even if My opinion on the financial health of the store is actually correct, it is still extremely unwise to conclude from this that the owner burned the store down to collect the insurance money. Tens of thousands of businesses go under every year in America, but commercial arson is very rare.

Now, let's add a little more information: the store that burned down didn't seem to be doing well. I'm sure it was torched by the owner for the insurance money. After all, he spent three years in prison at the end of the 90's hiring a man to burn down another store he owned.

Hmm.... this fact certainly makes My assumption that the owner torched the place look a lot less unwise, as the owner of the store has a history of commercial arson. Furthermore, while My inference is not nearly as impenetrable as it was before, it is still not entirely reasonable to conclude confidently that the store had been burned down. Many, many people who have been freed from parole after being convicted of conspiring to commit commercial arson never do that again.

Let's add a few more details: the store that burned down didn't seem to be doing well. I'm sure it was torched by the owner for the insurance money. After all, he spent three years in prison at the end of the 90's hiring a man to burn down another store he owned. On top of that, he owes $300,000 in gambling debt to some pretty unsavory characters. In addition, a number of local ex-cons told the police that the owner offered them money to burn down the place. He also took out commercial insurance policies last month with three different companies. And there's no getting around the fact that surveillance cameras from a nearby store show him carrying what looks like a gas can behind the store just before the fire starts.

These new details are completely changing things. Assuming all the information is true, is it still possible that the owner had nothing to do with the burning down of his store? Okay, it may be technically feasible, but it is virtually impossible for a reasonable person to believe. On the basis of the new information, it is not only reasonable to believe that he had torched the spot, it would be irrational to doubt it. The more proof I have that supports the argument that A triggered B, the more rational the conclusion is. At first, I had very little evidence to support the idea that the owner of the store had burned it down. However, as I have been presented with more evidence, the link between A and B has become almost indisputable. Of example, the cause and effect relationships you will find in the Logical Logical section will be somewhere between these two extremes, but you will use the same kind of reasoning process to evaluate them.

In many cases, the test preparers may connect a certain development of the evidence to the assumption that the evidence does not fully support it. The information given may be factual and reasonable up to a point, but somewhere in the argument, the examiners made a leap beyond the bridge they were building with the evidence— or loaded the bridge with more weight than they could support.

Consider this argument, remembering that you are only meant to determine whether, in this case, the argument supports the conclusion (regardless of your personal opinion on the subject): in the United States, more than six million middle and high school students read significantly below grade level. American fifteen-year-olds rank twenty-eighth out of forty countries in mathematics and nineteenth in science. Clearly, Americans don't spend enough on public education for their children.

For a multitude of reasons, many people would take this argument to face value, accepting the underlying assumption that all systems work better when they receive more financial support. That would be unfair, though, because there is very little evidence to support the inference. How much do I spend per student at the moment? How does that compare to what higher-ranking nations are spending on? How is that money allocated to the system? If the amount of money spent is not the problem, what are the other countries doing that I are not? Has my rating ever been higher, and if so, what have I been doing now that I are not? In short, is lack of funding essentially the primary cause of my poor score? If you were told that the United States is struggling for the first time in terms of student expenses, will you start looking for other causes? These are all questions that need to be considered before deciding that America does not spend enough on public education, and there are many more.

In the end, there may or may not be a correlation between the money I spend on education and the test scores my students receive. The idea is that embracing the claim allows you to make a huge mental leap in order to justify a conclusion that is not fully supported by the supporting statements. Please remember (again) that LSAT designers are banking on the fact that you will have a certain amount of unconscious bias in favor of a widely held view. They're taking advantage of this to try to keep you from noticing the logical relationships that have been left out. Most testers unwittingly supply missing logical connections as a result of personal bias and lazy reasoning, and thus answer the question incorrectly.

It is quite common in everyday verbal exchanges with others to pretend to know more than I do. There are a number of reasons why I do so, including a desire to avoid acknowledging ignorance of the subject at hand. We're not comfortable admitting that we're unable to connect all the dots that someone else presents as a complete picture.

Sometimes I fear that I may have missed something, especially if everyone else is nodding along in agreement, and I feel like we're the only one who doesn't know what's going on. You're having lunch with a group of friends in the dining room when another friend comes up and says, "Hey, man, have you heard Adele's new song? Isn't she the best one yet?" All your friends are chiming in about how much they love it, and you're nodding your head and making statements to the same effect, despite the fact that you didn't even know that Adele had a new single out. Some of your friends are probably faking it, too, for that matter. I all do this kind of stuff, and I do it all the time.

Okay, the ability can work in conversation, at least occasionally, but it won't get you anywhere on the LSAT. In reality, part of what is being evaluated in the Logical Reasoning portion of the LSAT is the ability to recognize and accept what you do not know — to be fully aware of missing links, disconnected information, and details that are unrelated to key issues, Take a look at the following example: Maude hates the city. She moved her family to Montana last year.

The connection of the statements makes it easy to conclude that Maude's reason for moving to a wide open state like Montana is her hatred of the city. But is that correct? Do you have enough evidence to conclude that this is the case?

Casually joining up the ideas in conversation is all right, but it's going to get you in trouble on the LSAT. Instead, consider the universe of facts that you don't know in this scenario. Using the example of a circle, everything I think fits inside the circle. What I don't know is all that's outside the curving line.

First of all, what I do know: Maude's strong disdain for the city where she moved, that she has a family of some kind, and a very general timing of the move.

What I don't know: this is a much, much longer list. Does it hate all cities or any particular city? Why does she despise (or despise) them? Was her move to Montana related to this preference or some other reason, such as a change of job or an urgent family situation? Is she trying to distance herself from someone else in a failed relationship? She's happily married, but she's searching for a lot of room for her seven kids to run around? Did she feel the urge to jump from state to state-literate, and she just finished Missouri? What is her family made up of (children, husbands, cats?) and does its relevance in this statement go beyond incidentals? I might, of course, go on and on.

The point is that there are many, many unknowns between the above two statements. Although some assumptions may be fairly reasonable given the information, and others may be of complete relevance, it is still important to understand that they are assumptions and are not, in fact, known.

Spotting Incomplete Arguments

One part of the LSAT problem that we're grappling with over and over is a claim that is somehow incomplete. This can lead to logical leaps and incorrect assumptions–filling in the blanks. For test preparers, any specific subject knowledge that you may have is substantially less important than the mental skills that you will use to identify the underlying assumptions and missing parts. So they're often deliberately pairing a statement with a conclusion that doesn't match the evidence, just to see how you deal with it.

First, you can put the skills described in Basic Concept #4 to bear: be mindful of what you don't know in a given scenario. Don't assume any facts. But hereIare going to take the ability one step further. Not only should you know what information is missing, you should also be able to identify the underlying assumption that you are trying to link the two. The following statement is presented to illustrate the point: Merla's fingernail was chipped, so she stopped in the library.

Yeah, yeah? In this case, it is clear that there is a missing link between the initial statement and the accompanying conclusion. What do the nails of Merla have to do with stopping at the library? IfIwere provided with additional information, such as that a nail-care seminar is taking place in the library, this might make more sense, but there is certainly no clear link between the two thoughts.

Nevertheless, it is doubtful that LSAT would use such an apparently unrelated pairing. Seek a more subtle example, as shown below: a well-educated citizenry is needed to maintain a free society. Robert has a perfect attendance at school, but he needs to be well educated.

As above, it's important to realize what you don't know first. It may be reasonable to suppose, or it may even be accurate, that Robert is well educated. You can not, however, deduce this with any certainty from the above-mentioned information. In addition,Iwould need to learn what is meant by good education, the steps involved in achieving one (presumably more than just turning up for school) and how Robert is behaving against those expectations.

One way the LSAT can test your ability to find incomplete arguments is by asking you to identify the assumption in the given passage. In this case, you would be looking for an answer choice: b. Consistent school attendance leads to good schooling.

LAternatively you might be asked which statement would most undermine the assumption behind the author's conclusion. In that case, something like this could be the correct answer: d. Some of the founders of Our nation, who were very learned men, have never formally attended school.

In the first place, define what is missing in the statement. It's easy to deal with the rest of the issue.

arts–a conclusion, and one or more premises. The assumptions are on which the author bases his inference. These are the facts or opinions that he expresses in support of his conclusion. The conclusion and the main point are always the same, so once you've come to the conclusion of the author, you've found his main idea. His main point is what he's trying to say, while his primary goal is what he aims to do by saying it.

Here's the statement that is part of the a "Main Point" issue.

Professional sports associations need to make some major changes if they want to stay in business. Drug use, violent crime, and irresponsible behavior have been rampant in the NFL, NBA, and MLB for years. It used to be that when people thought of professional athletes, they thought of great people like Willie Mays, Hank Aaron, Roberto Clemente, Oscar Robertson, and Walter Payton. Now they're more likely to think of Mark McGwire, Jose Canseco, Barry Bonds, O. J. Simpson, Ray Lewis, and Rae Carruth. If something isn't done to get people like this out of professional sports, a lot of fans will stop buying tickets.

What is the main point of the passage?

There are a lot of people in professional sports who have a bad character. People expect professional athletes to be role models for children. Pro sports leagues must take drastic action against the illegal and immoral actions of athletes. The use of steroids continues to be out of control in professional sports. Today's athletes do not possess the same moral quality of past generations of athletes.

The author clearly believes, and provides some evidence to support his belief, that there are a lot of people of bad character in professional sports. That's his main point, though? Let's not just make a decision yet, just keep going.

Does the author say that people expect professional athletes to be role models for children? No, it is not, although it is certainly a reasonable inference to something that the author believes. Of course, the main point of the author can sometimes be implied rather than clearly stated. However, although this seems to be something he'd feel very strongly about, it's certainly not his main point.

How about steroid use has been and continues to be out of control in professional sports, or today's athletes don't have the same moral quality of past generations of athletes. Obviously, the author strongly believes in the latter, and probably believes in the former, but does not specifically mention steroids; only drugs in general. At any rate, neither of them is his main point.

His main point is that pro sports teams must take drastic action against the illegal and immoral actions of athletes. This is almost a straightforward re-statement of the first sentence of the chapter, but not quite so. The first sentence says that professional sports groups need to make major changes if they want to stay in business, while the next section of the article deals with the illegal and immoral behavior of athletes. It is clear that the big improvements he proposes revolve around the bad behavior of the athletes. (By the way, in the Logical Reasoning section of the LSAT, the first sentence of the paragraph is often the inference of the speaker, although this is by no means always the case.) Inference Inference questions are also typical in the Logical Reasoning section of the LSAT. These are more complex than the Main Point questions, because these allow you to read between the lines or to add 2 and 2 together. They may ask you to determine what the author would agree or disagree with on the basis of the passage, even though there are no direct statements in the stimulus either for or against the position in the choice of answer. Or you might be asked what a fair reader would conclude from the passage, or what the author meant in the passage. Imply and infer, of course, are flip sides of the same coin–an author is implying something by suggesting it without saying it directly. A reader infers something by drawing a conclusion about something the author did not actually say, by making logical deductions from one or more of the things he said. Such questions can be posed in a variety of ways: would the researchers most likely agree with which of the following questions? The Senator would be least likely to agree with which of the following? The argument is most strongly supported by which of the following arguments? Which of the following can be properly inferred from the above passage?

Here's a statement followed by a standard Inference question: when you get right down to it, there are only two simple approaches to playing no limit hold 'em poker tournaments–long ball and small ball. Long ball is based on playing very few hands, but making big bets on either driving out opponents when bluffing or building a huge pot when holding a strong hand. Small ball players take the opposite approach—they get interested in a lot of games by making small bets before the flop, hoping to make a big hand and trap their rivals or trick them out of the pot with nothing. Both strategies have their benefits and their drawbacks. Choosing which one to use is a matter of personal preference.

The author would most likely agree that: The World Series of Poker Tournament has become too large and takes too long All poker players need to be skilled at both approaches to the game Long ball players tend to win more tournaments Small ball play is better suited to introverts Bluffing is a key skill to the success of the poker tournament.

How about all poker players need to be professional on both sides of the game? No; nothing like this is either stated or implied.

Does the author believe that long ball players tend to win more of the tournaments? No; if he believed that, why would he say that choosing a style depends on personal preferences? If the long ball approach led to more success in the tournaments, he would surely believe that this would be a crucial factor in choosing a playing style, and he would prefer that approach to the game.

Is the author likely to agree that small ball play is better suited to introverts? To date, this is the only answer that deserves any consideration at all. After all, the author says that the choice of playing styles depends on personal preference. Nonetheless, he says absolutely nothing to suggest that he assumes that a small ball is better suited to introverts. That response will make a lot of people go up because introverts tend to be shy and quiet, and the long ball style is very loud, so it's normal for our minds to think that the long ball style would be a poor match for introverts. Nevertheless, there is no clear link between personality and style of play, and since the author does not suggest that he sees any connection between the two, I can not infer that he agrees with this assertion.

Through elimination process, leaving bluffing is an essential skill for the success of the poker tournament, which is the correct answer. I know this is the right answer, because all the others are incorrect, but I can also test it using logical deductions. The author says that there are only two basic approaches to playing poker tournaments, and then he explains both, and both involve bluffing. In other words, there are no game types that do not include bluffing. It means he'd have to accept that bluffing is a key skill to the success of the poker tournament.

Underlying Assumption Another common question you will encounter in the Logical Reasoning exam will ask you to choose the answer that contains the assumption that the author is relying on to make his point. It is important to note that the presumption is not one of the assumptions mentioned by the author or the reasons given in support of his conclusion. In fact, the assumptions will never appear in the passage. Think of them as unwritten premises standing beside or behind the stated premises of the author, which are the reasons he gives in support of his conclusion.

For example, in the argument, the author can infer that D is based on C and B. Nevertheless, B or C simply hinges that A is real, even though the author never mentions A. So, A is the premise on which the author depends in order to make his case. It is important to keep in mind that assumptions are always undetermined, because on most of these types of questions at least one of the answers will be a slight rewording of one of the author's stated premises. It's going to be wrong, because if the author says something he's not saying, by definition. Even, while you will only be asked to pick one, there will always be many, many assumptions underpinning the case. Consider the following argument: O. J. Simpson is a killer, man. Murderers are not worthy of recognition and honor. Simpson should be removed from the Hall of Fame of the NFL.

Which assumptions does the author depend on? Several, in fact, but there are just a few: you can trust the media accounts of Simpson's activities just before and immediately after the murders of his ex-wife and his companion. Simpson was not framed for murdering racists in the Los Angeles Police Department. He was not framed for murder by a corrupt prosecutor's office.

The twelve jurors who found him not guilty were either incompetent or dishonest.

He (the author) has the power, at least in this case, to decide that someone is guilty of murder even though he has been absolved by a jury. Simpson is still in the Hall of Fame of the NFL. It's an honor to be in the NFL Hall of Fame.

We could go on and on, but there's a variety. These are all premises on which the author depends to be valid if his case is to hold water, even if he is not aware of all of them. If any of the above assumptions are wrong, his argument will fall apart.

That will always be the case if you have selected the correct answer to the Assumptions question–if the author's argument does not fall apart if the claim is not valid, then the answer is wrong.

Because at any point the argument is based on the assumption that if the presumption is turned on its head, the argument will fall apart.

Let's go back to the previous argument: professional sports leagues will make some major changes if they want to stay in business. Drug use, violent crime, and irresponsible behavior have been rampant in the NFL, NBA, and MLB for years. It used to be that when people thought of professional athletes, they thought of great people like Willie Mays, Hank Aaron, Roberto Clemente, Oscar Robertson, and Walter Payton. Nowadays people are more likely to think about Mark McGwire, Jose Canseco, Barry Bonds, O. J. Simpson, Ray Lewis, and Rae Carruth. If something isn't done to get people like this out of professional sports, a lot of people will stop buying tickets.

Which of the following is the assumption on which this argument is based?

A significant number of professional athletes are criminals or users of drugs. The Sports Commentaries

New Evidence Questions Another very common question type in the Logical Reasoning Test allows you to evaluate or rethink the statement in the light of new information. (This is the exact opposite of the Inference Questions, which allow the test taker to evaluate new information in the light of the argument.) There are a number of different forms of these new information questions in this portion of the LSAT. The two most popular are Strengthening Questions and Weaken Questions. They're coming in two kinds. The first type simply asks which answer choice supports or weakens the statement or conclusion. The second, however, asks you to choose the answer that most strengthens or weakens the point. In other words, you'll have two or three solutions that support / weaken the case in some way, and you'll need to pick the one that does it most effectively.

This second type of question is usually framed along these lines: which of the following, if true, reinforces the argument the most? Which of the following, if true, offers the most support for the conclusion? Which of the following, if true, weakens the argument the most? Which of the following, if real, most undermines the conclusion of the author? Each of the following, if correct, offers support for the EXCEPT argument: (this is obviously a weak question) You will see these kinds of questions on cases where the assumptions do not strongly support the inference. In other words, the proof is somewhat lacking–the assumptions make a case for the inference, but not one that is airtight and absolutely convincing. You will face five answers that each contain new information; at least one of them will certainly make the argument stronger or weaker, as the case may be.

It is important to note, however, that the extent to which the correct answer reinforces or weakens the argument can vary considerably. For one question, the correct answer could marginally harm the persuasiveness of the argument, while with another, the new information found in the correct answer might cause the argument to be completely dissolved. So the strength of the new information is not a matter of itself. It's only important when you have the most question, and new information in one answer is contrasted with new information in other answers. For example, if you're looking for the answer that most reinforces the argument, don't just choose the first answer that reinforces the argument in some way. It could very well be wrong, as there might be another answer that gives even more strength to the argument. Never forget the most about a question.

Keep in mind, too, that LSAT designers like to try out those kinds of questions by adding answers that contain information that seems strong and important, but in fact has nothing to do with the actual statement of the author, implying that it is actually completely irrelevant because it doesn't affect the argument at all.

Most Weakens Problem: Many people believe that advertisement plays a key role in deciding who to vote for in American presidential elections, but a recent study reveals that this assumption is a fallacy. I selected 5000 people, chosen from all 50 states in proportion to each state's share of the US population, and divided them into two groups. Participants in Group A each watched between 10 and 20 hours of television a week, while no one in Group B watched any TV at all. Three months before the last election, I asked each of them, in both classes, which presidential candidate they supported. Then, after the election was over, I asked each person they had voted for. At the beginning of the experiment, the members of Group A favored the Republican candidate by a margin of 51/49, but ended up voting for him by a margin of 56/44. Group B favored the Republican candidate by a margin of 52/48 at the start of the experiment, but by a margin of 57/43. Therefore, in both parties, the percentage of actual votes for the Republican candidate was exactly five percentage points higher than the level of support at the start of the study, and the level of support for the Democratic candidate was exactly five points lower, indicating that advertisement does not make a significant difference in the presidential election.

Which of the following, if valid, weakens the argument the most?

The total number of college years in both classes was exactly the same. The Democrats did not spend as much on TV ads as the Republicans did. Group B participants spent an average of 15 hours a week listening to the radio. Both candidates had high ratings of disapproval.

Two television stations in Alaska refused to publish any advertisements for political candidates.

Does the fact that the average number of years of college education in both classes was exactly the same undermine the argument? On the contrary, it would tend to strengthen it, since it reduces the likelihood that the demographic difference between the two groups will have an impact on the results.

Let's look at three of the remaining responses together: the Democrats did not spend as much on TV ads as the Republicans did.

The Democratic candidate has been tainted by a late-breaking scandal. Two television stations in Alaska refused to publish any advertisements for political candidates.

Is any of these undermining the argument? Despite the results of the study, it is not clear that the fact that the Democrats did not spend as much on TV ads as the Republicans did, was a major factor, although potentially it could have made a slight difference. If so, the case would be weakened. Let's just hold on to that comment.

Does the fact that the two candidates had high disapproval ratings undermine the argument in any way? No, it's not. In fact, this answer is totally irrelevant. I can reject this choice of answer out of hand.

Does the fact that two television stations in Alaska have refused to advertise for political candidates undermine the author's argument that advertising does not play a major role in how people choose which presidential candidate to vote for? It's very doubtful, as people in Group A have been proportionately spread across America. Alaska makes up a small percentage of the U.S. population, which means that very few (if any) members of Group A were affected by the lack of political ads on these two stations. So, while it could theoretically have had a tiny effect, it is very unlikely, and even less likely, that it would have had the impact that lower spending on the part of the Democrats might have had. So I can also discard this answer.

Let's look at the remaining option of answer. Would the fact that Group B members spent an average of 15 hours a week listening to the radio undermine the argument? Indeed, it would have been because it would represent a huge blind spot in the analysis. Experts seem to believe that the only way Americans can be subjected to presidential candidates ' advertisements is by watching television. However, since the claim does not stipulate that truth, I have no reason to assume that it is valid when evaluating the case of the author. Since it is common knowledge that radio stations air a lot of campaign ads during presidential campaigns, and there is nothing in the argument to the contrary, I can use this knowledge in My reasoning. When I do that, it's clear that it would logically follow that people listening to the radio 15 hours a week would hear a large number of presidential candidates ' advertisements. Since the author based the claim on the assumption that people in Group B were not exposed to presidential candidates ' advertisements, this knowledge demolishes his case, giving him the correct answer.

Lets try another one:

Some Strengthens Issue: Public awareness programs have reduced the number of alcohol-related traffic deaths in the US. One major factor in this decrease is the fact that many states now require people convicted of driving under the influence of alcohol to install interlocking ignition devices (breath analyzers) on their vehicles. Such systems make it impossible for a car to start when a person's breathing alcohol is detected. Nonetheless, even after decades of efforts to reduce drunk driving, tens of thousands of Americans are still killed every year by drunk drivers, so more needs to be done. Unless Congress passed a law requiring car manufacturers to include ignition interlock systems on every new vehicle sold in America, thousands of lives will potentially be saved every year.

Which of the following, if real, strengthens the argument the most?

The number of alcohol-related traffic deaths dropped sharply in the late 1980s, but has since been flattened.

Rapidly evolving technology makes it increasingly difficult for people to stop or beat interlocking ignition systems.

Because of the economies of scale, having all-vehicle interlocking systems would add less than $100 to the price of a new car.

Seven per cent of alcohol-related traffic deaths are caused by people previously convicted of driving under the influence of alcohol.

In a few years, iris recognition and vein matching technology will be incorporated into most interlocking ignition devices, providing prosecutors with extremely persuasive evidence in DUI cases.

D is the correct answer. Let's look at the answer choices in order: the number of alcohol-related traffic deaths dropped sharply in the late 1980s, but has since been flattened. Does that support the argument? No, no. The claim relies on the fact that, in this case, a law requiring breath analyzers on all new cars would save thousands of lives every year. This argument supports the sub-conclusion that more needs to be done about the number of road deaths, but does not support the idea that breath analyzers on every new car would save thousands of people's lives.

Rapidly evolving technology makes it increasingly difficult for people to stop or beat interlocking ignition systems.

That installing breath analyzers on all new cars is an effective way to dramatically reduce the number of people killed by drunk drivers.

Seven percent of alcohol-related traffic deaths are caused by people previously convicted of driving under the influence. This is the statement that, by far, does the most to strengthen the author's conclusion. How so? Well, if seven percent of alcohol-related traffic deaths are caused by people who have already been found guilty of driving under the influence that means that 13 out of 14 deaths are caused by drivers who have not previously been convicted of DUI, and therefore don't have interlock device on their vehicles. Since I know from the argument that interlock devices have been a major factor in reducing the number of traffic deaths from DUI, and nowIposit that at least 93% of the vehicles involved in DUI fatalities don't have one, it logically follows that installing them on all new vehicles would eventually dramatically reduce the number of drunk driving deaths in America.

In a few years, iris recognition and vein matching technology will be incorporated into most ignition interlock devices, giving prosecutors extremely persuasive evidence in DUI cases. Does this strengthen the argument in any way? No, it doesn't. The argument is about reducing the number of DUI fatalities, not about making it easier for prosecutors to convict people charged with driving under the influence. The statement neither strengthens nor weakens the argument; it is completely irrelevant.

Paradox Questions: For simplicity's sake, I referred to the reasons of the Logical Reasoning exam as arguments, but not all of them really are. Sometimes the stimulus will only pose a few facts without drawing a conclusion from those facts. If there is no conclusion in the text, there is technically no argument, and the stimulus is merely a reading passage. However, when referring to the Logical Reasoning passages in general, it would be very awkward to keep saying "arguments and facts sets" repeatedly, so whenItalk about the Logical Reasoning arguments in general,Ialso refer to those passages.

Paradox questions are taking this shape. Two or more facts are presented, and some of the facts seem to be at odds with each other, and the question will ask you to solve the problem by choosing the answer that resolves the paradox.

Paradox Problem Medical experts investigating the U.S. obesity epidemic have made an intriguing finding. With the cooperation of several restaurant owners, thousands of diners have witnessed and reported lunch over the course of several months. They found, as expected, that on average, seriously overweight people consumed far more calories while dining out than average-weight people did. However, when comparing calorie counts only among the seriously overweight diners, they were surprised to find that obese diners who were considered well-dressed consumed considerably less calories than those who were considered casually dressed at the same restaurant.

Which of the following statements, if valid, would provide the best explanation for the apparent paradox observed by the researchers?

Well-dressed diners tend to be more wealthy and can afford higher quality, less fattening food more easily.

In all weight categories, casually dressed people tend to eat more calories when they dine out than well-dressed people.

Casually dressed diners tend to be less educated and therefore less informed about what constitutes a healthy diet.

Well-dressed diners tend to be more image-conscious, so they eat less in public, but make up for it by eating more at home.

The researchers have had latent biases towards people who are overweight, and this has influenced their findings.

Before I look at the answer choices, let's look at the passage. Obesity researchers who have studied thousands of lunchtime restaurant patrons for several months have discovered what seems to be a paradox. What's that interesting finding? It's the fact that, on average, well-dressed obese people ate less calories than casually dressed obese people who weighed about the same.

What makes it a paradox? It's a (seeming) paradox, because one would reasonably assume that, in a study involving thousands of people, on average, people who weigh a certain amount would consume about the same amount of calories as other people of the same weight. However, among obese people of approximately the same weight, there was a significant difference in the caloric intake of well-dressed and casually-dressed people. Something's not going to add up here. How can casually dressed obese diners eat substantially more calories than well-dressed obese diners when weighing the same? It's up to you to decide which of the answers can solve the problem. Let's look at each of them.

Well-dressed diners tend to be more wealthy and can afford higher quality, less fattening food more easily. It makes perfect sense as a stand-alone argument. It is common knowledge that the lower the price, the more unsafe and fattening food tends to be when it comes to food. Keep in mind, however, that Iare not concerned with whether or not the statement in any of these answers makes sense, because for the purpose of answering the question, Imust accept it as true.

So, assuming the validity of this argument, does it do anything to solve the paradox? No, it's not. If well-dressed obese people eat only a few calories because they have the means to afford less fattening food, then why do they weigh as much as casually dressed obese people who don't have that option? So the question is still there, and the solution is wrong.

How about the next choice of answer? In all weight categories, casually dressed people tend to eat more calories when they dine out than well-dressed people. Is that the answer we're looking for? No, no. This simply takes one aspect of the equation–casually dressed obese people eat more calories while dining than well-dressed obese people do–and it extends to everyone in general, regardless of weight. While this suggests that casually dressed obese people eat more calories when dining than well-dressed obese people do is clearly part of a larger pattern that holds true across the board, it does nothing to explain why two groups of obese people with different eating patterns weigh about the same.

Casually dressed diners tend to be less educated and therefore less knowledgeable about what constitutes a healthy diet. This has a lot in common with A, and it's just as unsatisfactory when it comes to solving the paradox. Instead of implying that casually dressed people eat poorly because they can not afford to eat healthy food, the answer is that they eat poorly because they are not well educated enough to understand the principles of healthy nutrition. Although this may well be valid, there is simply nothing to solve the paradox. Because if well-dressed people make healthier food choices because they are better educated, why are they just as heavy as their less well-educated counterparts?

Well-dressed diners tend to be more image-conscious, so they eat less in public, but make up for it by eating more at home. Right off the bat, it looks more promising than the first three choices. Why? Why? Because it includes a factor outside the environment in which the researchers observed diners. That's in its favour, because logically, there are very few factors in the environment that could explain how two groups of people can weigh the same, despite significantly different patterns of calorie consumption. However, that doesn't necessarily make this the correct answer. I have to determine whether to solve the paradox. Sure, it does, and it's doing very well. Well-dressed obese diners eat less than their casually-dressed counterparts in restaurants because they are self-conscious about their image, but at home, when nobody watches, they eat enough to make up for themselves and the rest of the group. This explains the paradox of why both groups are quite nicely weighing the same thing. This is the correct answer.

The researchers have had latent biases towards people who are overweight and this has influenced their findings. Not only does this solution not clarify the paradox, it doesn't make any sense. However, since I are expected to grant the truth of the statement to see if it is right, let's think about it. Since the paradox involves two groups of overweight people, if the researchers had been predisposed to overweight, whether consciously or unconsciously, they would have been equally predisposed to both groups, which, in effect, would have meant that they would treat both groups almost the same way. So this statement does nothing to explain why there was a discrepancy between the groups. Had the researchers been predisposed to well-dressed people or casually dressed people, the aspect may definitely have played a role in the results, but the idea that they were predisposed to overweight explains little.

Keep in mind that the correct answer only needs to be the best explanation of the paradox of the five choices made. It doesn't have to be the best explanation theoretically possible. For example, it is certainly possible that the average well-dressed obese person is engaged in more exercise than his casually dressed counterpart. This might explain the paradox, and it might even be better than D above. It's not one of the choices, however. Of the five answers given, D offers the best explanation of the paradox.

Flawed Reasoning Questions: With most of the questions you will be asked about in the Logical Reasoning portion of the LSAT, the reasoning for the stimulus is basically sound. The author will not make any logical errors, and the conclusions will lead directly to the conclusion. Everything is going to work well together to form a solid case. But, that's not going to be the case with every stimulus. In some cases, the explanation used in the remedy will be illogical in some way, and the job will be to find out exactly what's wrong with the author's argument. Those are the Flawed Reasoning issues.

Sometimes the error is going to be quite easy to spot, but in a lot of cases it's going to be a lot more subtle. In fact, many times it's going to be so subtle that if it wasn't for the question that asked you to name the flaw, many people taking the LSAT would never realize that the reasoning was illogical.

(This is one of the main reasons that some people recommend reading the question before reading the stimulus, by the way. They say that if you know there's a rational flaw in the stimulus before you start reading it, you can look for it as you read it. They're right about it, but for other types of questions, it's better to read the stimulus first, and because the vast majority of questions about the Logica.

There are many different kinds of logical errors that the author may make, but they are all basically based on a false or unjustified assumption: reasoning from only one case to a large number of cases, confusing correlation with causation, believing that current conditions remain unchanged, imprecision in statistics or measurements, weak analogies, etc. You must always keep in mind that one or more of the answer choices are likely to be red herrings—one of those wrong answers that has been carefully and intentionally designed to trap you in choosing it as your answer. On Flawed Reasoning questions, LSAT designers often trip people up by offering one or two answers to choices that make reference to what the author actually does in the argument, but it's not illogical—it's actually valid reasoning.

Another common technique is to have one or more responses that respond to a common and well-known error of reasoning, but which is not part of the author's argument. For example, the answer could be that the author appeals to the authority or that the author assumed what he intended to prove when the author did not do such a thing. This second technique isn't as tricky as the first, but you should definitely be on guard against it, too.

Here is an example of the Flawed Reasoning question: it has been clearly shown that the average married man receives more income than the average single man. More than two hundred scientifically rigorous studies have been carried out on this subject, beginning almost fifty years ago and continuing today, by highly respected institutions such as Harvard University, Yale University and the University of Chicago. All told, these surveys involved millions of men from all levels of education across the country in hundreds of different professions, and each of them found that the average married man is paid more than the average single man. Obviously, there is widespread blatant discrimination in the labor market against men who are not married.

Which of the following best describes the flaw in the reasoning in this passage?

The claimant shall appeal to the authority to put his case to justice. The author assumes what he's supposed to prove. The author does not find other possible causes than prejudice. The author relies on insufficient or irrelevant information to make his case. The author does not use the exact figures for the average income.

Let's take a look at the argument and consider the answers.

The author points to over two hundred reports by highly respected organizations that compare the income of married men to the income of single men, all of which have shown that married men are paid more than single men. He points out that this happens across the board, to virtually every work and education level, across the world, and has been going on for a long time. He states that single men are discriminated against by employers.Iknow from the question that his reasoning has a flaw.Ineed to determine what the flaw is. Is it that the author appeals to the authority to make his case? It sounds promising. A well-known logical falsity is the appeal to the authority, and the author relies on studies for his evidence, and points out that some of them have been conducted by elite universities. So he's certainly guilty of making a logical fallacy appeal to the authority, isn't he? Well, not that easy. While this would lead to a large number of test takers, it is not the correct answer.

While the author references a variety of sources, he does not make an appeal to the fallacy of the authority. Some people who have heard that appeal to authority is a logical fallacy seem to think that one can never cite the authority to back up the argument. This is nonsense; these people do not understand the absurdity of the authority's appeal. Appealing to an authority is only a logical fallacy if the authority has no experience in the topic under review or if many other similarly competent authorities do not agree on the matter.

For example, if I have an argument about Roman Catholic theology, and you quote a well-known Catholic theologian to back up your point, that is not a logical fallacy, because a Catholic theologian would certainly understand Catholic theology. However, if we're talking about which baseball player was the biggest ever and I say, "It's Babe Ruth because my priest said so," then I've made an appeal to the authority's fallacy. Only an appeal to an authority outside the subject matter, or a quotation from one authority on a subject which is disputed between experts on the subject, are logical flaws. It's perfectly logical to quote the authorities who know what they're talking about. So the answer is wrong.

Is the author assuming what he's supposed to prove? This is another logical falsity, formally known as asking the question. Here's a simple argument that begs the question: Cigarettes are not healthy because they're bad for you. This argument begs the question because the conclusion is nothing but a re-statement of the premise. Like a little boy who claims his dad's always right, and his friend asks him how he knows, and the boy responds, "Because Dad said so," that's what's known as a circular argument. Does the author make this logical error? No, he's not. His premise that married men make more money than single men is not the same as his conclusion that employer discrimination against single men is the cause of disparity.

How about the author's inability to consider other possible causes than discrimination? Okay, this one sounds like it might have some validity. Because it is the LSAT , Ihave to assume that the facts in the author's premise are correct, and that hundreds of studies have shown that married men make more money than single men as an irrefutable fact. Does it necessarily follow, however, that prejudice against single men on the market is the cause of this? Are there any other factors that could possibly cause this phenomenon?

Could experience not be one factor that might be involved? Older men are more likely than younger men to be married, and older men are more likely to have more experience than younger men. Because employers usually favor employees with more experience to those with less experience, it seems reasonable that they would pay more. Another possible factor is motivation–doesn't it make sense for a man with a wife and/or children to be motivated to work longer hours than a single man and thus earn more income? These are just two possible explanations of pay disparity that do not involve discrimination, and the author did not consider either one, let alone any other. So that's the correct answer.

What about the author relying on insufficient or irrelevant data to make his case? Why is that wrong? Well, if only one research had been listed by the scientist, he wouldn't have had much of a case. Alternatively, he pointed to more than 200 studies by elite universities, involving millions of men from all walks of life, in hundreds of jobs, over a 50-year period, all of which came to the same conclusion. Assuming that the facts cited by the author in the stimulus are true, asImust do in the case of the LSAT, it is clear that there are sufficient, relevant data to establish a scientific consensus on this issue.

The author's failure to use accurate figures on average income is true, but completely irrelevant. The 200 + studies have shown that there is a pay disparity between single and married men, and they argue that the mere existence of the disparity, not its size, is proof that there is widespread discrimination against single men in the workplace. Nothing in the argument requires a statement of the exact figures.

Parallel Reasoning These questions are very common in the Logical Reasoning section of the LSAT, and you should expect to see some of them when you take the exam. They may be more difficult to answer correctly than many of the other types of questions, so they usually eat up more of the clock you're racing against. That's because, with Parallel Reasoning Questions, you're not just analyzing one argument; you're analyzing six–each choice of answer is an argument, too. Because of this, we're going to spend more time discussing these issues than we've spent on other types of issues.

On Parallel Reasoning Issues, the stimulus will be a very concise argument, with only a few lines. Upon digesting the statement, you will be asked to read the five answer options, and to pick the one that includes the argument that most closely resembles the stimulus justification. LSAT designers have a number of ways to phrase this, but they're all very similar, so there's no question that you're dealing with a parallel reasoning problem. Analyzing and comparing five reasons to the original that take quite a bit of time, and this is another explanation why some LSAT guides suggest that you read the question before reading the stimulus. I suggest skipping all of the Parallel Reasoning questions, and only coming back to try them after answering all the other questions first.

It's your call, of course, but I think you're going to do better if you stick toMyadvice to read the stimulation first. As one thing, you're not going to have to read the question to determine that you're looking at the parallel explanation question. That's going to be clear, because the incentive is going to be a statement that's just a paragraph or too long. However, for that very reason, first reading the stimulus won't take a lot of time, so how much time would you have saved anyway?

This is not to suggest you should never miss a topic and come back to it later. Sometimes that might be the wisest approach for you to take. This depends on how complex the problem is. Some of the Parallel Reasoning problems are pretty hard to untangle, but, actually, many are not that hard. If you get bogged down on one of these questions, skip ahead by all means and just come back to it if you've answered all the other questions. (You should always skip ahead if you get seriously stuck on any question on the LSAT, no matter what kind of problem it may be.) It is not advisable, though, to have a general policy that you will skip all the parallel reasoning issues until the end, because many of them are not particularly difficult. Since other kinds of questions can also be very complicated, you could very well miss a question that you could easily answer just to run into another question that totally stumps you.

As the name implies, the correct answer to the Parallel Logic questions will follow the same logic found in the original statement. In other words, the two statements must be identical in their logical structure. If the original argument is analogous, the correct answer will contain an analogy. If the stimulus relies on circular reasoning, the correct answer will also be given. If the original argument is inductive, you will be looking for an inductive argument in the choice of answer.

In some instances, the form of reasoning used in the claim is not all that clear or easy to distinguish, but that is usually not a problem. The much larger problem is that some of the solutions will be so close, or so ambiguous, that determining which one is best suited to the logic in the original argument seems to be a job whose complexity lies somewhere between splitting hairs and reading goat bowels. You will need to analyze and compare some aspects of the two claims in order to find the correct answer.

Validity is the first element. Sometimes the stimulus argument is valid, in which case the correct answer must also contain a valid argument. Sometimes the trigger statement involves a logical flaw. In that case, the correct answer statement must also be invalid. You'll be able to know for sure if the stimulus argument is valid or invalid, because if it's invalid, the question stem will say so. If the question stem does not use a word such as defective, illogical, or questionable to describe the stimulus argument, the argument is valid.

Don't put too much weight on validity, however. It's definitely a requirement, but it's just one factor that you need to consider when looking for parallel reasoning. Or, to put it in formal logical terms-that the correct answer must match the validity or invalidity of the original argument is a necessary but not sufficient condition. Besides, it is very unlikely that, as the case may be, only one answer option will be valid or invalid.

Next, you'll want to compare the conclusions of each argument. Remember, the stimulus and the five response choices are all arguments, so all of them must have conclusions (and at least one premise). The conclusion in the correct answer would have much in common with the conclusion in the original argument. This does not mean that the subject matter is going to be the same or similar. Nor does it mean that the two arguments must have the same place of conclusion with respect to the premises. Premises could come before the conclusion in the stimulus, and after the conclusion in the answer (or vice versa), and they could still be a match.

Two of the parallels you are searching for in the findings are variety and assurance. These are the language functions used in the statements. If the conclusion in the stimulus contains broad, all-encompassing absolutes such as all, must, must, must, never, etc., then the conclusion in the correct answer must have the same scope, even if it is not expressed in exactly the same way. Compare, for example, these two conclusions: people over the age of 50 never win a marathon. No one over the age of 50 will ever win a marathon.

They both say the exact same thing, even though only the first one never uses the word, and one sentence refers to people, while the other one uses a person. Such results are therefore a match.

So draw these two conclusions: people over the age of 50 will never win a marathon. People over 50 hardly ever win a marathon.

Are these two assumptions going to say the same thing? No, it's not. The first is an utter, categorical declaration that a person over the age of 50 will never win a marathon. The second one says it's rare for anyone over 50 to win a marathon, but it doesn't say it's never going to happen. These assumptions are not true.

So scope or scope is a very important clue when determining the correct answer to parallel reasoning questions. The certainty is another factor that needs to be considered. Remember these two conclusions: eating too much can cause you to have diabetes. Smoking cigarettes is going to stain your teeth.

In the first, it is mentioned that A may possibly lead to B, while in the second, it is assumed that A certainly results in B. One conclusion is certain, while the other is indefinite, so these conclusions are not the same. There is, of course, quite a bit of overlap between specificity and certainty; the important thing to keep in mind is to look for any kind of absolute. If the conclusion of the stimulus is absolute, then the correct answer must also be given. If the result of the original argument has an infinite extension, the answer containing the absolute is incorrect. Because the conclusions must match the scope / certainty, it is often the case that the argument in the correct answer contains some of the same words or phrases as the original. This is not always the case, and it should not be viewed on its own as a smoking gun level of proof, but it can definitely be an important clue.

So, get to grips with these questions by first seeing if the method of reasoning jumps at you. If so, you will usually be able to choose the correct answer without further examination. If this is not the case, consider the validity of the argument and delete all the answers that do not match the valid argument. If you're still not sure, compare the conclusions for scope and certainty. In most situations, if you need to compare the results with a view to deciding the correct answer, this should be enough to encourage you to choose the winner. However, if you are still unsure, compare the stimulus premises with the response choices premises, using the same principles as described above. If you're still not sure of the correct answer after that, then it's probably time to move on to another question.

Here's a taste of Parallel Reasoning Question: Great college professors love to read. Bob has over a thousand books on his e-reader, so he's going to make a great college professor.

The wrong reasoning in which one of the following arguments most closely parallels the wrong reasoning in the above-mentioned argument?

People with analytic minds are good at chess. Everyone in the accounting department is of an analytical mind. Zelda works in the accounting department, so she's going to make a good chess player.

All baseball players can learn how to switch-hit if they train long enough. Jose Ramirez was the MVP of the American League last year, so he'd be able to master the switch-hitting in just a few weeks.

Everyone who works for an airline loves to travel. Derek has been a airline booking clerk for seven years, so Derek loves to travel.

When the sky is red in the morning, it normally rains at the end of the day. The sky is red this morning, so it's going to rain later.

The best restaurant managers would like to cook. Zoe is throwing some terrific dinner parties, so she'd be a very good restaurant manager.

Let's take a deep look at this.

First of all, why is this claim flawed? It's illogical because the fact that great college professors enjoy reading doesn't mean thatIcan assume that all people who love reading are great college professors. In other words, loving reading is a necessary condition for being a great college professor, but it is not a sufficient condition.

Is A the correct answer to that? In other words, does it have the same faulty reasoning as the stimulus argument?

Individuals with logical minds are good at chess. Everyone in the accounting department is of an analytical mind. Zelda works in the accounting department, so she's going to make a good chess player.

Let's just break it down. It boils down to all members of A being B, and all members of C are members of A, and D is a member of C, therefore D is a member of B. Is this logic incorrect? No, it's not; it's totally valid. There's an extra step in there that might potentially turn some people away, but it's a perfectly logical statement. It can not therefore be correct, as the correct answer must contain incorrect reasoning.

Moving to B: Both baseball players can learn how to switch-hit if they train long enough. Jose Ramirez was the MVP of the American League last year, so he'd be able to master the switch-hitting in just a few weeks.

Is that argument valid or invalid? It's invalid—while the premise is that all baseball players can learn to switch hits, there's nothing that says that the faster the player learns, let alone the time limit on the learning curve, the better the player learns. This argument is based on the

How to take a practice LSAT

A practice test is not just another homework assignment. It is an important opportunity for you to get as accurate a picture as possible of your readiness to earn a score that will make you proud. Your results will help you make informed decisions about your prep schedule and keep your study sessions productive.

Full timed practice tests give you insight into areas that will be critical to your success on Test Day: did you run out of time in any of the sections?

- Have you been nervous?
- Have you been hungry?
- Have you got thirsty?
- Did you get sick of that?
- Have you been able to stay focused?
- Have you survived 3.5 hours of waking up without looking at your phone?

Use a paper pad for sketches and diagrams Use a No. 2 pencil—you'll need one for a paper test on Test Day, and it's a good idea to use one when you take the test online, too.

Warm Up Eat a healthy dinner the night before the practice test, including slow-release energy carbohydrates (for example, rice, pasta, potatoes). It's a mental marathon— but you're supposed to fuel your body and mind as if you're running a real one.

Get a good night's sleep (at least 8 hours) Wake up no later than 7:00 a.m.— that's how it's going to be on Test Day Saturday morning, so try doing it the same way for a practice test if you can!

Eat a healthy breakfast (for example: coffee, fruit, eggs, pancakes, toast— nothing too sugary!) Be prepared Use real paper to write the sample-you'll write it by hand on Test Day!

Number 2 Pencils and paper for diagrams and other notes Water and healthy snacks on hand-your kitchen won't be next to the Testing Site!

Location and Environment If possible, take a practice test in a library— not at home comfort No distractions!

Turn off your phone and leave it in your bag If you need to use your phone as a timer, put it in Airplane Devices On Test Day mode, you will not be allowed to access your phone or any other electronic device at all— not even during breaks — or your scores may be cancelled. Don't do that during a practice test! For these 3.5 hours, you need to know what it feels like to be disconnected.

Get Started If you are taking the September / October, December or February administration test in the US, you must report to the test center no later than 8:30 a.m., so do your best to start your practice test around that time. The June LSAT reporting time is 12:30 p.m.

More FAQs on the LSAC website Note: Just so you know you're anticipating it, on Test Day, you're likely to sit quietly in a tense room with prospective law students for half an hour or so before the test actually starts! For part of that time, you'll be filling out the forms and listening to the instructions. You will also sign a statement that swears that you are the one you say you are.

Top tips:

Do the essay: Don't forget to compose a sample of writing–after three hours of testing, you need to know what it feels like to do with this task.

Be truthful with yourself: give yourself the exact amount of time indicated for each segment. Don't allow yourself a few extra seconds to fill in the bubbles with questions you haven't been asked yet. If you do that on Test Day, your scores may be cancelled.

Take Official Breaks: Take a 15-minute break after the third multiple-choice section. This is it. It's alarming.

Stay hydrated and energized: eat healthy snacks and drink water during your breaks Test your practice test Here are some helpful questions to consider while evaluating your performance: did you sleep at least 8 hours in the night before the practice test?

- Have you woken up at least one hour before the practice test?
- Have you eaten a healthy breakfast?
- Have you been happy with your breakfast? Would you like to try another kind of breakfast food next time?
- Have you started the test at 8:30am?
- Did someone take the exam for you?
- Have you used a written test sheet and a bubble disk?
- Have you taken one sitting?
- Have you allowed yourself a test day break (one 15 minute break after the third multiple-choice section)?
- Did you drink any water during the breaks?
- Did you eat healthy snacks during the break?

Have your snacks made you happy? Treat yourself during the break—you should only eat healthy and happy snacks!

Now I will leave you with some practical advice about the day of the exam. The best way to prepare is by practicing test questions (coming up!). Try to treat each one like a real exam. Practice the conditions of the day (as best you can) so that you are not caught out.

I have some final tips/pointers about the last things to do before and exam, below. use these tips in your practice tests, and in the real thing. And good luck!

The 10 best study tips and tricks for the night before the exam

It's the night before the big exam. The hard work is done, your preparation has come to an end, and now is the ideal time to calm down your nerves and make sure that you're ready to enter the exam hall well rested and confident in your ability to write an outstanding exam essay.

1. Play it safe: One of the first rules to run a marathon is not to do it in new shoes. The principle of 'nothing new' in sporting events applies to food, apparel, habits, and so on. If you haven't done anything in the past, it's not time to experiment with new memorization methods, pharmaceuticals (legal or illegal) or job habits. Go with what worked best in the past, no matter how much someone might try to convince you of a newer, better, or faster way. And this includes how much of the advice you might want to take.
2. Ready well in advance There's an old adage that says,' Well started is half done.' Even before you spend the night before the exam is up, you should also spend the days before the night before you get dressed. The night before the test, it's not time to hunt down the book from the library that your professor insisted on reading at. Everything you need to prepare for the exam should be available for use the night before so that you can make the most of your time.
3. Sleep is a friend of yours Most people think that the best use of their study time is to sacrifice sleep so that they can study more. Yet study after study shows that having enough rest is key to the way you process new information. I suggest this: come home and take a little nap before you continue your studies (20-30 minutes). Start fresh, then. Get a regular night's sleep for 6.5-8 hours, but go to bed early. Then start studying the first thing again when you wake up until it's time to take the exam. This will give you two opportunities to re-energize the material. If you skip to sleep, you'll never really feel fresh, and most likely you'll just feel irritable, distracted, and burned.
4. Eat right. You want to eat healthy, with a nice mixture of good carbs, proteins and fats. It might be best to avoid a massive carb that's just going to make you sleep with a sugar crash, especially on the morning of the exam. Probably the best way to avoid taking too much caffeine as well. Drink plenty of water to help the brain function optimum. You want to get the most out of your food and drink, but you don't want to use it to popular your returns. However, as always.
5. Be an examiner One of the most effective ways to prepare for an exam is by actually taking an exam for yourself. Go through all your materials (textbooks, notes, ancillary materials) and look for questions. Suppose that you are the most cruel and sadistic interviewer to have ever existed. Then take the test. It will definitely give you an idea of where your strengths and weaknesses lie.

6. Study groups and study buddies There is a very high chance that you are not the only one preparing for the same exam the night before. Find someone or a group of people you trust to stay on the job and want to do well and study with them. It's best to arrange this ahead of time, but this can be a very effective way to prepare for an exam. It makes the best sense, however, to keep the number small and to work with people who might be slightly more efficient than you are in class.
7. Go offline (scary but necessary) Unless there is an important, study-related reason you need to be linked to Instagram, Snapchat, TikTok, and so on, you can consider dropping the face of the virtual world for a few days. It might start with the need for Google to name something that might be on the exam and end up two hours later with you laughing at a cat video and hating how you got sucked down another rabbit hole. For the 12-24 hours leading up to the test, the only thing you need to concentrate on is the exam. Everything else could be waiting.
8. Limit distractions and contacts Getting off the Internet, or just turning off your computer, is limiting your distractions. Those, sadly, could be a few. Today, of course, there are people who actually think and work better with the noise around them. But what we're talking about here is the distraction that will suck up the time needed: your housemate who wants to recount last night's antics, a friend who wants to hit the stores with you, your mom who won't stop calling... If best you can, be inaccessible until the exam is over.
9. As far as structuring your time goes, you can't do any worse than the famous Pomodoro productivity model. This method has been developed by Francesco Cirillo and is based on the little red tomato kitchen timers. Essentially, work one thing with the timer set for 20-25 minutes. Then take a short break (stretch your legs, get a drink). Then go for another 25 minutes. Take a long break for 15-30 minutes after 4-5 sets of 20-25 minutes. Then continue again. The most important part of this method is that you focus entirely on the task at hand for those 20-25 minutes. But, as always, see #1.
10. Be ready to go: The closer you get to the next day, and definitely the next morning, the more nervous you get, and potentially the more oriented you get to the test. On the day before your test, I suggest that you get everything you need in advance. Have your clothes ready to wear (and better go with layers in case the room is too warm or too cold). Have what you're going to eat more or less ready to eat. It's probably best to have a shower the night before. This way, you won't have to make too much effort to get ready in the morning.

Go to the exam room prepared, concentrated and relaxed. Good luck, this is what you have!

Good Luck, now try these practice tests.

Test 1

Section 1 Analytical Reasoning – final questions missing answers

Time: 35 minutes for 25 questions

Directions: Each group of questions in this section is based on a set of conditions. In answering some of the questions, it may be useful to draw a rough diagram. Choose the response that most accurately and completely answers each question and blacken the corresponding space on your answer sheet.

Questions 1–5 refer to the following scenario.

A a number of women and men are attending the United States convention in support of women's rights in Seneca Falls, New York. Six prominent feminists and abolitionists will speak at this meeting: Emma, Liam, Ava, Isabella, Sophia, and Martha. Each of them will speak once and only once, and only one person speaks at a time. One person speaks per hour; the first speaker begins at 2 and the last one at 7. The following rules determine the order in which they speak:

Neither Liam nor Isabella may speak at 6.

Sophia speaks before either Liam or Isabella but not before both.

If Ava speaks at 2, then Emma must speak after Martha.

If Sophia speaks at 4, then Martha speaks at 7.

1. Which one of the following could be an accurate order of speakers?
   A. Liam, Ava, Sophia, Isabella, Martha, Emma
   B. Liam, Sophia, Emma, Martha, Isabella, Ava
   C. Ava, Isabella, Emma, Sophia, Martha, Liam
   D. Ava, Martha, Liam, Sophia, Emma, Isabella
   E. Martha, Sophia, Ava, Frederick

2. Liam, Emma, Isabella 2. If Ava speaks at 2, then which one of the following must be false?
   A. Emma speaks at 5.
   B. Liam speaks at 3.
   C. Isabella speaks at 3.
   D. Martha speaks at 4.
   E. Martha speaks at 5.

3. If Martha speaks at 7, then which one of the following must be true?
   A. Ava speaks at 4.
   B. Sophia speaks at 4.
   C. Isabella speaks at 5.
   D. At least one person speaks before Ava speaks.
   E. At least two people speak before Liam speaks.

4. All of the following speakers can speak at 2 EXCEPT:
   A. Emma
   B. Liam
   C. Isabella
   D. Sophia
   E. Martha

5. Which one of the following could be an accurate partial schedule of speakers?
   A. Emma at 3; Sophia at 6
   B. Ava at 2; Sophia at 3
   C. Ava at 2; Martha at 7
   D. Martha at 3; Sophia at 4
   E. Sophia at 5; Emma at 7

Questions 6 - 11 refer to the following scenario.

Seven famous chefs — Charlotte, Mia, William, Jacques, Elijah, Marthe, and Mason— have volunteered their services for a presidential dinner. It consists of five courses, served in the following order: hors d'oeuvres, consommé, entrée, salade, and dessert. The dinner begins at 7 and ends at 10. One or two courses are served each hour, at 7, 8, and 9. The chefs refuse to work with one another, so each course is prepared by exactly one chef. No chef can prepare more than one course per hour. The following chefs have offered to prepare the following courses:
Hors d'oeuvres: Mia and Marthe
Consommé: Charlotte and Elijah
Entrée: Charlotte and Nigel
Salade: Mia, William, and Jacques
Dessert: William, Elijah, and Marthe

6. What is the minimum number of chefs who could prepare the entire meal?
   A. two
   B. three
   C. four
   D. five
   E. six

7. If the salad is served at 9, which one of the following could be a complete list of chefs who prepare a course served at 8?
   A. Charlotte and Elijah
   B. Mia
   C. William and Nigel
   D. Elijah
   E. Marthe

8. Which one of the following CANNOT be a complete and accurate list of the chefs who prepare the meal?

A. Charlotte, Mia, Jacques, and Elijah
B. Charlotte, Mia, Elijah, and Marthe
C. Charlotte, William, Marthe, and Nigel
D. Charlotte, Jacques, Elijah, and Marthe
E. Mia, William, Jacques, and Marthe

9. Which one of the following pairs of chefs could each prepare two courses served during the same two time slots?
A. Charlotte and Mia
B. Charlotte and Elijah
C. Charlotte and Marthe
D. Mia and William
E. Elijah and Nigel

10. Which one of the following pairs of chefs could each prepare a course served at 7 and a course served at 9?
A. Charlotte and Elijah
B. Charlotte and Marthe
C. Mia and Elijah
D. Mia and Marthe
E. William and Marthe

11. Which one of the following could be a complete and accurate list of the chefs who prepare the meal?
A. Charlotte, Mia, William, and Nigel
B. Charlotte, William, Jacques, Elijah, and Nigel
C. Mia, William, Elijah, and Marthe
D. Mia, William, Marthe, and Mason
E. William, Jacques, Elijah, and Marthe

Questions 12-17

A Doctor will see patients in two different hospitals from Monday to Friday of next week. Patients A, B, C, D, and E are in hospital 1, and patients R, S, T, U, and V are in hospital 2. The Doctor sees only one patient from each hospital per day, but the Doctor sees two patients per day. The order in which the Doctor sees patients is governed by the following:
A is seen on the same day that R is seen.
C is seen on the same day as T.
V is not seen on the same day as D or E.
A is seen before C.
S is seen after C.

12. If A is seen on Wednesday, then which of the following could be true?
A. D is seen on Monday with V.
B. V is seen after S.
C. B is seen on the same day as U.
D. D is seen on Friday with S.
E. T is seen on a day before V.

13. If B is seen on Wednesday, then which of the following must be true?
A. A is seen on Tuesday or Monday.
B. D is seen before B.
C. E is seen on the same day as S.
D. D is seen on the same day as U.
E. A and B are seen on consecutive days.

14. If B is seen on Friday, then which of the following must NOT be true?
A. D is seen on the same day as V.
B. A is seen on Monday with R.
C. V is seen on Friday with B.
D. R is seen after the day that U is seen.
E. C and T are seen on Wednesday.

If C is seen on Tuesday, then which of the following could be true?
A. D is seen with V on Wednesday.
B. S is seen on Monday or Tuesday.
C. B is seen on Friday with S.
D. Neither D nor E is seen on the same day as S.
E. E is seen on Friday with U.

15. If V is seen on Tuesday and D is seen on Wednesday, then which of the following must be true?
A. E is seen on Friday with S.

B. D is seen with S on Wednesday.
C. A, B, and C are seen on consecutive days
D. A is seen on Tuesday.
E. U and S are seen on consecutive days.

If B is seen the day after the day that S is seen, then which of the following could NOT be true?

A. V is seen the day after E is seen.
B. U is seen the day after D is seen.
C. E is seen the day after A is seen.
D. D is seen the day before A is seen.
E. T is seen the day before U is seen.

Questions 16–18

A total of six pieces of fruit are found in three small baskets: one in the first basket, two in the second basket, and three in the third basket. Two of the fruits are pears—one Bosc, the other Forelle. Two others are apples—one Cortland, one Dudley. The remaining two fruits are oranges—one navel, one Valencia. The fruits' placement is consistent with the following:

There is at least one orange in the same basket as the Bosc pear.

The apples are not in the same basket.

The navel orange is not in the same basket as either apple.

16. Which of the following could be an accurate matching of the baskets to the pieces of fruit in each of them?

A. basket one: Forelle pear basket two: Dudley apple, navel orange basket three: Bosc pear, Cortland apple, Valencia orange
B. basket one: Dudley apple basket two: Bosc pear, navel orange basket three: Forelle pear, Cortland apple, Valencia orange
C. basket one: navel orange basket two: Cortland apple, Bosc pear basket three: Forelle pear, Dudley apple, Valencia orange
D. basket one: Valencia orange basket two: Cortland and Dudley apples basket three: navel orange, Bosc and Forelle pears
E. basket one: Valencia orange basket two: Bosc pear, navel orange basket three: Forelle pear, Cortland and Dudley apples

17. Which one of the following CANNOT be true?

A. A pear is in the first basket.
B. An apple is in the same basket as the Forelle pear.
C. An orange is in the first basket.
D. The oranges are in the same basket as each other.
E. Neither apple is in the first basket.

18. Which one of the following must be true?

A. An apple and a pear are in the second basket.
B. An orange and a pear are in the second basket.
C. At least one apple and at least one pear are in the third basket.
D. At least one orange and at least one pear are in the third basket.
E. At least one orange and at least one apple are in the third basket.

Questions 19–25 refer to the following scenario.

On a Friday afternoon, an English literature student rents from the local library five film versions of literary classics — Emma, Great Expectations, Ivanhoe, Middlemarch, and Wuthering Heights — to help him prepare for an exam the following Friday morning. Three of the films are on disc and two are on videotape. The student can watch no more than one film per evening, and Thursday is the last night he can watch a film. The student must schedule his film viewing under the following conditions:

Emma is on videotape. Wuthering Heights is on disc.

The student must watch Wuthering Heights before he watches Emma.

The student must watch Middlemarch and Ivanhoe after he watches Great Expectations.

The student must watch Emma on Monday. The student cannot watch any two videotapes on consecutive days or any two discs on consecutive days.

The student must watch a film on disc on Saturday.

19. Which one of the following could be an accurate schedule of the student's viewing of the films?

   A. Friday:Great Expectations; Saturday: Wuthering Heights; Sunday: Emma; Tuesday: Middlemarch; Wednesday: Ivanhoe
   B. Friday:Great Expectations; Saturday: Wuthering Heights; Monday: Emma; Tuesday: Middlemarch; Wednesday: Ivanhoe
   C. Friday: Great Expectations; Saturday: Wuthering Heights; Monday: Emma; Tuesday: Middlemarch; Thursday: Ivanhoe
   D. Friday: Wuthering Heights; Sunday: Great Expectations; Monday: Emma; Tuesday: Ivanhoe; Wednesday: Middlemarch
   E. Saturday: Wuthering Heights; Monday: Emma; Tuesday: Middlemarch; Wednesday: Great Expectations; Thursday: Ivanhoe

20. If the student watches Great Expectations before he watches Emma, then which one of the following statements CANNOT be true?

   A. Great Expectations is on disc.
   B. Ivanhoe is on disc.
   C. Middlemarch is on disc.
   D. The student does not watch a film on Sunday.
   E. The student does not watch a film on Wednesday.

21. If Middlemarch is on videotape, then which one of the following statements could be true?

   A. Ivanhoe is on videotape.
   B. The student watches Emma exactly three days before watching Middlemarch.
   C. The student watches Great Expectations exactly one day before watching Middlemarch.
   D. The student watches Ivanhoe on Wednesday.
   E. The student watches Middlemarch on Thursday.

22. Which one of the following statements must be false?

   A. The student watches films on both Friday and Monday.
   B. The student watches films on both Monday and Wednesday.
   C. The student does not watch a film on either Friday or Sunday.
   D. The student does not watch a film on either Sunday or Wednesday.
   E. The student does not watch a film on either Tuesday or Thursday.

23. If the student watches Great Expectations after he watches Wuthering Heights, then

which one of the following statements must be false?
- A. The student does not watch a film on Friday.
- B. The student watches Ivanhoe before he watches Middlemarch.
- C. The student watches Great Expectations before he watches Emma.
- D. Great Expectations is on disc.
- E. Ivanhoe is on disc.

24. If the student does not watch a film on Wednesday, then which one of the following statements must be true?
- A. The student watches Great Expectations on Friday.
- B. The student watches Great Expectations on Tuesday.
- C. The student watches Ivanhoe on Tuesday.
- D. The student watches Ivanhoe on Thursday.
- E. The student watches Middlemarch on Tuesday.

25. If the student watches Ivanhoe before he watches Middlemarch, then how many different ways could he schedule his list of films to view them all during the week?
- A. one
- B. two
- C. three
- D. four
- E. five

Section 2 Logical Reasoning

1. A recent news story featured a runner whose shoes caught fire just as the runner completed a 100-meter dash. An attendant near the track quickly put out the fire with a fire extinguisher. The story indicated that the friction of the shoes on the track had sparked the fire, but after thinking about it, I questioned why someone would be ready with a fire extinguisher near a track. It must have been a publicity stunt because the runner claimed that this had never happened before.

1. Which of the following is the main point of the passage?
  A. The friction from the track did not cause the runner's shoes to catch fire.
  B. The fact that the running shoes caught fire was nothing more than a publicity stunt.
  C. Runners faster than this runner have never had their shoes catch fire after a race.
  D. The news network did not reveal the publicity stunt because it attracted more viewers.
  E. The runner's feet were not burned by the fire.

2. All trees in the Coconino National forest are hardwoods. All squirrels living in hardwood trees have fluffy tails or matted tails, but not both. All squirrels in the Coconino National forest live in hardwood trees in the Coconino National forest. Which of the following can be concluded from this passage? All squirrels have fluffy or matted tails.
  A. Squirrels who live in the Coconino National forest never climb softwood trees.
  B. Squirrels without tails are present in the Coconino National forest.
  C. No trees in the Coconino National forest are softwoods.
  D. All shrubs in the Coconino National forest are hardwoods.

3. I. Cars produced by French companies tend to be more durable than cars produced by American companies. II. The average life of a car made by an American company is about five years longer than the average life of a car made by a French company. Which of the following, if true, would explain the discrepancy noted in the passage above?
  A. Cars produced by French companies tend to have longer lifetimes than they do in France or in the northern parts of America.
  B. Car specialists would prefer to use a French refrigerator in their offices and an American car in their homes.
  C. French cars are made from more durable parts than American cars.
  D. People buy only cars made by companies in their country, and the French subject their cars to greater levels of stress than Americans do.
  E. Certain people would like to falsify records regarding average car life in order to gain an edge for national trade.

City elections are a trying time for all candidates. Voters peruse the life histories, opinions, and personalities of the candidates in order to determine who is best suited for office. Knowing that they have been so carefully scrutinized by the public, candidates can be extremely disheartened if they lose. Some candidates never get over the sense of rejection that comes with losing the race. However, candidates should understand that, in most cases, they are competing with equally qualified and worthy opponents. Recognizing the strength of the competition, candidates should not feel rejected when they lose.

4. Which of the following is the main point of the passage?

    A .City elections should be decided based on the strength of the candidate pool instead of a person's subjective opinions.

    B .City elections are places where voters choose between several credible candidates in order to determine who is best suited to govern their city.

    C .Candidates should be less competitive because they are all trying to do the same thing: elect the person who would best serve the interests of the city.

    D .Mature candidates realize that getting elected is difficult, and they are not disappointed if they happen to lose.

    E .Elections are difficult times for candidates, and losers should use perspective when interpreting their losses.

Tool commercials are famous for appealing to wit and humor in order to sell their products. Tool brands try to associate themselves with a carefree nature that takes on the world and then laughs at it after the world has been won over. This illusion of dominance is something that all men crave, so a tool that appeals to this attitude is bound to be successful. Tool marketers understand this fact, acknowledge it, and use it to produce some of the most compelling advertisements on TV.

5. If the claims of the passage are true, then which of the following can be concluded?

    A .Commercials that appeal to males' illusion of dominance are generally successful.

    B .Less tool would be purchased if tool was not so heavily advertised.

    C .Humor is a good way to market all products.

    D .Tool marketers can also make commercials that cater to women's illusions.

    E .An advertisement's success is determined by the number of products it sells.

6. Even though the brain patterns of infants are qualitatively different from the patterns common to adults, it is helpful to study infant brain patterns because they give insight into how adult brain patterns develop. Additionally, research on infant brains makes evident a sort of neural progression that accompanies the process of maturing. Specific infants have unusual brain patterns that do not resemble the normal infant pattern, and while these infants do receive some attention from scientists, they do not receive nearly as much attention as the groups of infants with normal infant brain patterns. Which of the following, if true, would explain why infants with idiosyncratic brain patterns do not receive a lot of attention?

    A .Nothing can be determined about neural development by studying infants with unusual brain patterns.

B. Infants with normal brain patterns and normal development schemes tend to be much cuter than infants with abnormal patterns.

C. Abnormal brain patterns hold the key to understanding the brain pattern progression extending from childhood to adulthood.

D. Scientists tend to look for idiosyncrasies when studying groups of infants, but not when studying adults.

E. Infants with idiosyncratic brain patterns develop into adults with normal brain patterns.

7. Lucas: Moving is an incredibly exhausting process. Surely all of my energy is not sapped just by moving boxes. I feel as though I am forcefully extricating myself from a past life every time I move. I am probably as emotionally tired as I am physically exhausted. Wanda: Extracting yourself from your previous home is hard and tiresome. It is just as much an emotional venture as it is a physical one. What is the main point of Lucas's argument?

A. Moving is an exhausting process.

B. Moving is emotionally and physically tiring.

C. Moving boxes is the most tiring aspect of moving.

D. Lucas is moving from a good point to a worse point.

E. Wanda should have been helping Lucas to move instead of watching television.

8. Scientists have found that disorders of the immune system are not caused by psychological factors; instead they are caused almost entirely by physiological factors. Yet numerous statistical accounts support the fact that people being treated for stress by psychologists are much more likely to have immunological disorders than are members of the general population. Which of the following, if true, would resolve the paradox presented in the argument?

A. A psychological problem that causes stress is not generally known to contribute to immunological disorders.

B. Immunological disorders cause many psychological problems, one of them being stress.

C. The presence of doctors tends to dramatically increase the level of stress in a person who is being measured for stress level.

D. People without immunological disorders tend to be more stressed during the times when they believe that they have a disorder than during the times when they do not believe this.

E. Numerous rare elements have been discovered that would contribute not only to a person's stress level but also to diseases affecting the immune system.

9. Koi ponds are an excellent addition to any backyard. Koi can grow to about 3 feet in length, and in a large enough pond, they will spawn more koi. Each individual Koi has vibrant color patterns and can live for decades, if taken care of properly. If you have a pond that is big enough, all of your koi will live to be at least 15 years old. Which of the following must be assumed in order to properly draw the conclusion?

A. Koi are better pets for children than dogs are because most children are unable to swim with their dogs.

B. Koi keep their color patterns until they are at least 15 years old.

C. If your pond is big enough, a heron will not eat one of your koi when it is 5 years old.
D. Koi cannot live in a pond that is big enough in some environments.
E. Koi will not eat each other when they reach the age of 25.

10. Politician: It is wrong for a government to infringe upon the liberty of an individual, except in those cases when to fail to restrict a person's liberty would directly result in another person being harmed. However, no ethical or legal statement may well be made regarding the responsibility of a government to protect a person from harming him- or herself; such a responsibility falls to that person alone. Which one of the following can be properly inferred from the politician's statements?

A. It is wrong for an individual to harm him- or herself.
B. It is not morally wrong for a government to make suicide illegal.
C. A government should interfere with a person's liberties only when that person's actions will lead to harm of any sort.
D. A person may legally harm him- or herself as long as no one else is harmed.
E. It is always wrong for a government to restrict an individual's liberties.

11. Restoration of medieval artwork often revives the original colors, posing a dilemma for art historians. Modern interpretations of medieval art have been based on pre-restoration colors and must now be reevaluated. Which of the following principles, if valid, most helps to justify the reasoning above?

A. Art interpretation must be done during the period in which the artwork is created.
B. Restoration of a piece of art can alter the colors used by the artist, rendering the artist's vision invalid.
C. The best judges of the worth of a piece of art are art historians.
D. The colors used in a work of art are a significant factor in the interpretation of that work.
E. Art interpretation varies due to the period in which the interpretation is made.

12. Valentine's Day is the most difficult day of the year for people who are not in love. A holiday that was maniacally crafted by candy makers, card makers, and florists to sell their products has exacerbated feelings of loneliness in all the single members of our society. To change this situation, we must unite to refuse to buy candy or send cards to anyone this Valentine's Day. By doing so, we serve the greater good of eliminating this holiday once and for all. Which of the following is an assumption upon which this argument relies?

A. Valentine's Day is a holiday that serves no purpose besides making people feel lonely.
B. The government would be served by eliminating Valentine's Day as a holiday.
C. Holidays cannot be unmade by people in the same way that they were made by corporations.
D. The negative effects associated with Valentine's Day outweigh any positive effects of the day.

E. Valentine's Day will not be eliminated as a holiday by any effort made by anyone.

13. Logan never lost a baseball game. I believe that it was because he would wear his hat backwards while pitching. The sort of bold, brazen attitude that was manifested by his backwards hat seemed to fluster his opponents. I remember how the children in that little league would wither under his gaze even before he threw his pitches. However, it could also have been his baggy pants that signaled his rebel attitude. I have never really been sure myself, but regardless, those children must have been intimidated by his attitude, because he never lost a game that he pitched. Which of the following if true would tend to support the conclusion of the passage?

A. Baggy pants signaled Logan's rebellious attitude just as much as the backwards cap did.

B. In terms of pitching mechanics, talent, and skills, Logan was the worst pitcher in the little league.

C. No pitchers in the little league won all their games except those who wore their hats backwards.

D. Baseball games are not affected by the style or even the attitude of the pitcher.

E. Logan was drafted last year by the New York Monsters, an upcoming professional baseball team.

14. In a study of centenarians, it was shown that there were several commonalities among people in the group. First, each person exercised moderately, going on walks of at least an hour five times a week. Second, none of them consistently used any mind-altering substances like alcohol, tobacco, or any other more serious drug. Lastly, many people gardened. Scientists are uncertain of the effect of gardening on a person's longevity, but apparently it is profound, because otherwise the centenarians as a group would not have been doing it so consistently. To increase my chances of living past 100, I will begin gardening today. Which one of the following is an assumption on which the conclusion is based?

A. Taking long walks and abstaining from harmful substances promote good health, and gardening is an inspirational activity.

B. Moderate exercise combined with gardening and abstinence from harmful substances will cause a person to become a centenarian.

C. Old age was not the sole reason so many in the centenarian group were gardeners.

D. Scientists will not be able to develop a pill that can confer on people the positive effects of gardening.

E. There are no factors that contribute to a person's longevity besides those listed.

15. Psychologist: There has been a long-standing debate concerning the implications of nurture versus nature in a person's development. A person's "nature" refers to the set of genes inherited from the person's parents, and a person's "nurture" corresponds to the environment in which a person lived while growing up. More than likely this debate will never cease, because it is impossible to separate the effects of nature from those of nurture on a person's development. But someday this argument will end, not because a solution has been found or a consensus reached, but solely because people are without exception tired of arguing

about it. Which of the following, if true, most undermines the conclusion of the passage?

A. Although the nature-versus-nurture debate has raged for years, the leaders of each camp have never come to an agreement.

B. Ten years after the psychologist wrote this passage, a solution to the debate was found by a premier German biologist.

C. The truth is that both nature and nurture influence development in a synergistic rather than unilateral fashion.

D. In 50 years, 75% of society will believe that nurture is the factor that is mostly responsible for a person's development.

E. Most people are already tired of the nature-versus-nurture debate, and more than likely this unconcerned percentage will increase in future years.

16. Millions of people throughout the years have relied on the assumption that in winter the weather gets colder and in summer it gets warmer. It appears, however, that this assumption is wholly unfounded. Dr. Spock, a noted climatologist, stated in a speech earlier this year that the climate change associated with changing seasons is nothing more than an illusion. It makes sense, therefore, that there is really no such thing as a discrepancy in the average temperatures between the different seasons. The major flaw in the reasoning of the passage is that it

A. assumes that a traditional view is incorrect on the basis of an appeal to a unilateral authority in that field

B. ignores the possibility that there will be no correlation between the past and the future

C. relies merely on the opinion of millions of people over many years.

D. engages in a type of syllogistic reasoning that is uncommon and not in accord with clear scientific tradition

E. confuses evidence in support of a certain conclusion with evidence in support of a different conclusion

17. The coach should have realized that making his son captain of the team was immoral. It is wrong to let a child make decisions for a team just because he is the coach's son, so it is also wrong for a large group of team members that includes the coach's son to make decisions for the team. Which of the following contains reasoning that is flawed in the same way as is the reasoning in the argument?

A. Actors should not be allowed to be in movies solely because they are attractive people. People who are spontaneous should be in movies in addition to actors who are attractive.

B. Sports players should not be allowed to gain commercial sponsorships solely because of their natural athletic abilities. Therefore, it is wrong for a large group of people to gain commercial sponsorship when a sports player is not included in the group.

C. The coach's sons are the two captains of the team, and this situation is wrong because other people wanted to be captains. Therefore, other people should be captains besides the coach's sons.

D. Animals should not be relegated to the outskirts of our society solely because they are not human. Therefore, impoverished people in our society should not be relegated to the outskirts of our society.

E. The rich should not be allowed to make all political decisions solely because of their wealth. Therefore, it is wrong to include any rich people in the governmental body that makes political decisions.

18. Miriam: Scientists claim that dogs can hear high-pitched noises better than all other mammals. This is certainly true in respect to cats. Yesterday I blew my high-pitched dog whistle right next to my cat, but she did not twitch a muscle. However, this contention does not apply to bats. Last night, I blew the same whistle outside when a group of bats was eating bugs near the streetlamp. The bats heard the whistle, started shrieking, and flew away. The argumentative technique Miriam employs to refute the opinion of the scientists is to

A. use the scientific method to determine whether dogs hear high-pitched noises better than bats

B. elucidate an implicit contradiction in the scientists' logic

C. supply clear evidence that would refute the scientists' claim

D. misinterpret the meaning of the key term hear when testing the scientists' theory

E. point out the existence of a group that scientists might not have examined

19. Questions 19 and 20

Giant Market Gains Advertising Representative: Salon Harperbegan advertising with Giant Market Gains at the beginning of last month and has seen a 27% increase in sales. It is clear that placing ads with Giant Market Gains can dramatically increase your company's sales. Each of the following, if true, would weaken the advertising representative's conclusion EXCEPT:

A. Noah's Ark pet shop advertises with Giant Market Gains and has never matched the monthly sales of Salon Isabella.

B. Giant Market Gains only serves a small portion of Meinhart County.

C. Last month was a holiday month, when business is typically higher than average.

D. Zane, an internationally famous stylist, joined the staff of Salon Harperlast month.

E. Last month, Salon Harper offered a discount on their spa packages.

20. The advertising representative's conclusion would be most strengthened if it were true that

A. Giant Market Gains is delivered to homes on a weekly basis.

B. Salon Harper did not change any of its products or services last month.

C. The Giant Market Gains ad included a coupon for a free paraffin wax treatment when a manicure is purchased.

D. Salon Harper has decided to continue advertising with Giant Market Gains.

E. Last year, Salon Harper did a direct-mail ad and saw no significant increase in sales.

People who treat others worse than they would like to be treated tend to incur the fury and disdain of the person who has been badly treated. People who treat others better than they like to be treated tend to be taken for granted and eventually rejected. Based on these findings, it appears that a person should follow the Golden Rule: Treat others as you would like to be treated. The application of this age-old rule will facilitate positive interactions in our society. Children should be taught this rule in preschool so that they will unerringly adhere to its wisdom as adults.

21. The argument above is vulnerable to which of the following criticisms?

    A. It makes a conclusion that is unrelated to the passage.
    B. It supports a contention by negating a premise that rejects that contention.
    C. It derives a general principle from a limited number of supporting claims.
    D. It forges a conclusion based on an appeal to morality without a correlative appeal to logic.
    E. It constricts the application of a rule that should be implemented.

Wireless networking has changed the electronic format of college campuses. Computers can access the Internet from more places, making it more reasonable for students to have laptop computers. Students can log on to the Internet when they are bored in class. Networks can be built that exchange files between computers within a certain distance of each other. As wireless networking gains ground, it will continue to mold our college campuses.

22. The argument makes use of which of the following argumentative methods?

    A. It makes a conclusion that is dramatically broader than is warranted.
    B. It offers contradictory evidence in support of a singular premise.
    C. It makes an assumption based on a nonrepresentative group of people.
    D. It delineates examples to support a specific claim.
    E. It eliminates several competing premises in favor of a superior premise.

23. A well-known histamine blocker is known to decrease the incidence of allergies in its users by 10%. The incidence of allergies in a local nursing home has been decreased by 10%, so patients there must be using the histamine blocker. Which of the following contains the same flawed reasoning as the passage above?

    A. Whaling has been determined to decrease the population of whales by 15% each year. The whale population has decreased by 15% this year, so whaling must be the culprit.
    B. Weightlifting has been determined to increase the performance of individuals up to 15%. The performance of a high school basketball team has increased by 15%, so players must have started weightlifting.
    C. Injury is likely to decrease a joint's effectiveness by 15%. John's joint is 15% less effective than it was before, so he must have injured it.
    D. Heart attacks strike 15% of people in their old age. Therefore, 15% of people in this nursing home will have a heart attack.
    E. Watching sports is a pastime that 15% of American households engage in all day Sunday. People in this household have watched television all Sunday, so they must have been watching sports.

24. Brain surgeon: The feeling of nostalgia is triggered by a portion of the brain that does

not trigger any other type of emotion. Most emotional responses result from the activation of synapses in one particular cranial region, but nostalgia is activated by synapses in an isolated subdorsal cranial region. Searching for a reason that accounts for this discrepancy has led me to hypothesize that nostalgia is not a real emotion, that it is an emotion that develops later in life than any other emotion, or that it is the result of something unexplained in our evolutionary history. Since nostalgia has to be a real emotion, it follows that it must develop later in people's lives than all other emotions. A flaw in the passage is that it

A. Assumes that a temporal sequence in the evidence implies a causal relationship

B. Draws a conclusion without first eliminating all possible competing solutions

C. Misinterprets the key term emotion when formulating the conclusion of the passage

D. Appeals completely to emotion when a scientific theory is evaluated

E. Provides no evidence in support of an obvious contention that would disprove the conclusion

25. Stuntman: I prefer car crashes to motorcycle crashes, because in a car crash, I have a shield of metal protecting me from the ground and other vehicles. Motorcycle crashes are more dangerous because there is nothing to protect me. Jumping out of burning buildings is the worst, though, because then I don't even have a bike—only a trampoline cushions my fall.

Daredevil: I like jumping out of burning buildings best because it makes me look cool. After that, I like motorcycle stunts because they increase the likelihood of getting into an accident that will really test my body's limits. Car crashes are too dangerous since there are so many other people and vehicles involved.

The daredevil and the stuntman are committed to disagreeing about which of the following?

A. Car crashes are more dangerous than motorcycle crashes.

B. Jumping out of burning buildings makes people look cool.

C. The more vehicles involved in an accident, the more dangerous it is.

D. The less metal to shield a person's body in an accident, the more dangerous it is.

E. Stuntmen often do not use trampolines to cushion their falls from burning buildings.

Section 3 Reading Comprehension

Time—35 minutes

25 questions

Directions for Reading Comprehension Questions: Each passage in this section is followed by a group of questions. Answer each question based on what is stated or implied in the passage. For some questions, more than one answer choice may be possible, so choose the best answer to each question. After you have chosen your answer, mark the corresponding space on the Answer Sheet.

The stored communication portion of the Electronic Communications Privacy Act (ECPA) creates statutory privacy rights for customers of and subscribers to computer network service providers. In a broad sense, ECPA "fills in the gaps" left by the uncertain application of Fourth Amendment protections to cyberspace. To understand these gaps, consider the legal protections we have in our homes. The Fourth Amendment clearly protects our homes in the physical world: Absent special circumstances, the government must first obtain a warrant before it searches there. When we use a computer network such as the Internet, however, we do not have a physical "home." Instead, we typically have a network account consisting of a block of computer storage that is owned by a network service provider, such as America Online. If law-enforcement investigators want to obtain the contents of a network account or information about its use, they do not need to go to the user to get that information. Instead, the government can obtain the information directly from the provider.

Although the Fourth Amendment generally requires the government to obtain a warrant to search a home, it does not require the government to obtain a warrant to obtain the stored contents of a network account. Instead, the Fourth Amendment generally permits the government to issue a subpoena to a network provider that orders the provider to divulge the contents of an account. ECPA addresses this imbalance by offering network account holders a range of statutory privacy rights against access to stored account information held by network service providers.

Because ECPA is an unusually complicated statute, it is helpful when approaching the statute to understand the intent of its drafters. The structure of ECPA reflects a series of classifications that indicate the drafters' judgments about what kinds of information implicate greater or lesser privacy interests. For example, the drafters saw greater privacy interests in stored e-mails than in subscriber account information. Similarly, the drafters believed that computing services available "to the public" required more strict regulation than services not available to the public. (Perhaps this judgment reflects the view that providers available to the public are not likely to have close relationships with their customers, and therefore might have less incentive to protect their customers' privacy.) To protect the array of privacy interests identified by its drafters, ECPA offers varying degrees of legal protection, depending on the perceived importance of the privacy interest involved. Some information can be obtained from providers with a mere subpoena; other information requires a special court order; and still other information requires a search warrant. In general, the greater the privacy interest, the greater the privacy protection.

1. The primary purpose of the passage is to
   A. qualify and explain the purpose of ECPA
   B. argue that the Fourth Amendment alone is not enough protection in our age of technology
   C. exalt the brilliance of the drafters of the ECPA
   D. describe the difficulty of obtaining a search warrant for information in cyberspace
   E. debate the ethicality of network service provision

2. Using inferences from the passage, the author would be most likely to describe the attitudes of the public network service providers referenced in line 42 as
   A. ignoble
   B. impious
   C. pompous
   D. clandestine
   E. indifferent

3. The author argues that the ECPA is an important reinterpretation of our right to privacy because
   A. subpoenas are extremely easy to obtain
   B. public network service providers have very little incentive to protect their customers' rights, especially if the providers can make a profit
   C. the greater the need for privacy, the more protections the ECPA tends to provide
   D. as our personal information becomes more likely to be stored in a nonphysical realm, the Fourth Amendment alone has a decreasing power to protect it
   E. the complicated nature of the statute allows it to be interpreted in many different ways, depending on who wants to use it in their favor

4. According to the author, the Fourth Amendment had what kind of effect on cyberspace privacy rights before the ECPA?
   A. momentous
   B. ambiguous
   C. incendiary
   D. progressive
   E. adverse

5. The author most likely mentions that "our homes [are] in the physical world" (lines 11–12) in order to
   A. offer a place where there are gaps to be filled in the Fourth Amendment by the ECPA
   B. remind the reader of the difference between a real home and a "cyber" home
   C. explain why there is less incentive for government officials to pursue obtaining personal data from computer memory when it is far easier to get a search warrant for a physical home
   D. address the contrast between the relative simplicity of protecting a physical object as opposed to the uncertain protection of computer memory
   E. distinguish our homes from the homes of government workers

6. The passage provides support for which of the following claims?
   A. The drafters of the ECPA were some of the most popular legislators in America.
   B. Personal e-mails are legally considered more private than personal account information.
   C. It is considered less important to protect privacy in computing services available "to the public" than in those that are "private."

D. In our modern age, the Fourth Amendment is outdated and could be generally disregarded without effect.
E. Network service providers have given the government a great deal of legal trouble with reference to privacy rights over the past several years.

Russia is the largest of the 15 geopolitical entities that emerged in 1991 from the Soviet Union. Covering more than 17 million square kilometers in Europe and Asia, Russia succeeded the

Soviet Union as the largest country in the world. As was the case in the Soviet and tsarist eras, the center of Russia's population and economic activity is the European sector, which occupies about one-quarter of the country's territory. Vast tracts of land in Asian Russia are virtually unoccupied. Although numerous Soviet programs had attempted to populate and exploit resources in Siberia and the Arctic regions of the Russian Republic, the population of Russia's remote areas decreased in the 1990s. Thirty-nine percent of Russia's territory, but only 6% of

its population, in 1996 was located east of Lake Baikal, the geographical landmark in south-central Siberia. The territorial extent of the country constitutes a major economic and political problem for Russian governments lacking the far-reaching authoritarian clout of their Soviet predecessors.

In the Soviet political system, which was self-described as a democratic federation of republics, the center of authority for almost all actions of consequence was Moscow, the capital of the Russian Republic. After the breakup of the Soviet Union in 1991, that long standing concentration of power meant that many of the other 14 republics faced independence without any experience at self-governance. For Russia, the end of the Soviet Union meant facing the world without the considerable buffer zone of Soviet republics that had protected and nurtured it in various ways since the 1920s; the change required complete reorganization of what had become a thoroughly corrupt and ineffectual socialist system.

In a history-making year, the regime of President Mikhail Gorbachev of the Soviet Union was mortally injured by an unsuccessful coup in August 1991. After all the constituent republics, including Russia, had voted for independence in the months that followed the coup, Gorbachev announced in December 1991 that the nation would cease to exist. In place of tmonolithic union, there remained the Commonwealth of Independent States (CIS), a loose confederation of 11 of the former Soviet republics, which now were independent states with an indefinite mandate of mutual cooperation. By late 1991, the Communist Party of the Soviet Union (CPSU) and the Communist Party of the Russian Republic had been banned in Russia, and Boris Yeltsin, who had been elected president of the Russian Republic in June 1991, had become the leader of the new Russian Federation.

Under those circumstances, Russia has undergone an agonizing process of self-analysis and refocusing of national goals.

That process, which seemingly had only begun in the mid-1990s, has been observed and commented upon with more analytic energy than any similar transformation in the history of the world. As information pours out past the ruins of the Iron Curtain, a new, more reliable portrait of Russia emerges, but substantial mystery remains.

7. Which of the following best describes the main idea of the passage?
   A. In its transition to self-governance, Russia, unlike the other 14 republics, has been shaken by controversy, political failure, and stubborn remnants of the corrupt Soviet regime.
   B. Corruption among the Communist leadership was the sole problem in Soviet politics, but in the end it was enough to dissolve the Union.
   C. Russia's strength relies on the full exploitation of its resources, and the Soviet Union's inability to tap into Siberian riches led to its downfall.
   D. Russia's political remodeling since late 1991 has been one of the most studied transformations in history.
   E. Over the past several years, Russia's rapid emergence from a corrupt socialist system has required political transformations on a colossal scale.

8. Which one of the following would Russian politicians probably deem the most detrimental contributor to Russian politics before 1991?
   A. the Russian Federation
   B. Boris Yeltsin
   C. Europe
   D. Communism
   E. self-governance

9. The phrase "monolithic union" in line 56 most likely refers to
   A. a metaphor comparing the Soviet Union to obdurate stone
   B. the massiveness and perceived indestructibility of the Soviet Union in late 1991
   C. the way that the republics together comprised a single association and acted as a uniform block
   D. the Soviet leaders' tradition of demonstrating their power by building huge statues that were displayed around the republics
   E. a popular nickname the stalwart Mikhail Gorbachev acquired due to his physical build and political obstinacy

10. The second paragraph primarily serves to
    A. explain why the effects of the breakup of the Soviet Union meant that the new republics would need to entirely reconstruct their political systems and attitudes
    B. offer several reasons why the 15 republics were better off in the long term as part of the Soviet Union
    C. describe the short-term goals of most of the republics just after the breakup of the Soviet Union
    D. blame the collapse of the Soviet Union on Communism
    E. argue that the 15 republics were far better off when the center of authority was in Moscow

11. It can be inferred that most Russian citizens view Siberia as which of the following?
    A. intolerably inhospitable
    B. politically overwhelmed
    C. unfairly exploited

D. favorably desolate
E. uncomfortably overpopulated

12. According to the passage, all the following are true of Russia since its emergence from the Soviet Union EXCEPT:
   A. it has had to deal with the loss of control of the satellite republics that constituted its buffer zone
   B. it banned Communist parties from the country
   C. it has attracted the attention of many social scientists, historians, and cultural analysts
   D. it underwent a very difficult political transformation
   E. it has developed into a corruption-free, benevolent political entity

Stem cells have recently become an important focus for scientific research around the world. They have two important characteristics that distinguish them from other types of cells. First, they are unspecialized cells that renew themselves for long periods through cell division. Also, under certain physiologic or experimental conditions, they can be induced to become cells with special functions such as the beating cells of the heart muscle or the insulin-producing cells of the pancreas.

Scientists primarily work with two kinds of stem cells from animals and humans: embryonic stem cells and adult stem cells, which each have different functions and characteristics. Scientists discovered ways to obtain or derive stem cells from early mouse embryos more than 20 years ago. Many years of detailed study of the biology of mouse stem cells led to the discovery, in 1998, of a means to isolate stem cells from human embryos and grow the cells in the laboratory. These are called human embryonic stem cells. The embryos used in these studies were created for infertility purposes through in vitro fertilization procedures, and when they were no longer needed for that purpose, they were donated for research with the informed consent of the donor.

Stem cells are important for living organisms for many reasons. In the 3- to 5-day-old embryo, called a blastocyst, a small group of about 30 cells called the inner cell mass gives rise to the hundreds of highly specialized cells needed to make up an adult organism. In the developing fetus, stem cells in developing tissues give rise to the multiple specialized cell types that make up the heart, lung, skin, and other tissues. In some adult tissues, such as bone marrow, muscle, and brain, discrete populations of adult stem cells generate replacements for cells that are lost through normal wear and tear, injury, or disease. It has even been hypothesized that stem cells may someday become the basis for treating diseases such as Parkinson's disease, diabetes, and heart disease.

Scientists want to study stem cells in the laboratory so they can learn about their essential properties and what makes them different from specialized cell types. As scientists learn more about stem cells, it may become possible to use the cells not just in cell-based therapies but also for screening new drugs and toxins and understanding birth defects. Current research goals include both determining precisely how stem cells remain unspecialized and self-renewing for so long and identifying the signals that cause stem cells to become specialized cells.

13. The author's primary purpose in writing this passage was to
   A. argue the necessity for an effective diabetes treatment and oppose the use of mouse embryonic stem cell research
   B. aggressively defend the ethicality of gathering embryonic stem cells from human embryos
   C. hesitantly debate the role stem cells will most certainly play in future medicine
   D. offer a relatively new-age alternative medicine therapy as a possible treatment for several persistent diseases
   E. explain stem cell research in relatively basic terms and point out its greatly untapped potential

14. According to the passage, the hypothesis, given in the end of the third paragraph, that stem cells hold the key to treating some of the most troublesome diseases of our time would suggest which of the following?
   A. Stem cell research will provide the means for several preventive therapies, which could be put in place in a developing fetus.
   B. Research in the field of stem cells is rapidly nearing its limit of applicability.
   C. Cells that have already become specialized are of little use when it comes to disease treatment.
   D. Many more stem cell donors will be needed to supply the cells needed for all the upcoming research.
   E. Stem cell research could prove more important in the medical world than anyone could have possibly anticipated.

15. Which one of the following statements is best supported by the properties of stem cells listed by the author?
   A. A single cell may originate as a stem cell, but it could still live the majority of its life span as a muscle tissue cell.
   B. Stem cells embody the peak of evolutionary achievement.
   C. Embryo donors are vastly decreasing in numbers as legislation is passed against these sorts of infertility procedures.
   D. Birth defects are most often caused by improper differentiation of cells from stem cells.
   E. Stem cells can be gathered from only embryos or cadavers.

16. Which one of the following statements, if true, lends the most support to the author's argument that stem cell treatments will become a valuable staple in the medical world in years to come?
   A. Currently, stem cells are considered relative mysteries of science, but many researchers still believe in their promise.
   B. Stem cells multiply without any contact inhibition, much like cancer cells.
   C. Though stem cells have much potential as a new form of medical treatment, there is doubt whether we will ever be able to efficiently manipulate them.
   D. By inducing stem cells to differentiate into the tissue of choice, doctors can use healthy new cells to replace an afflicted patient's damaged or diseased cells.
   E. There is no need for any more embryo donors for the harvesting of stem cells

because they renew themselves indefinitely.

17. Which one of the following can replace the word essential in line 54 without significantly changing the author's intended meaning?

A . auxiliary
B . fundamental
C . necessary
D . superfluous
E . unique

18. Which one of the following best describes the organization of the passage?

A . A topical theory is offered, the author supports the theory with mundane evidence, and then he or she concludes by calling the reader to action using emotional persuasion.
B . Clashing hypotheses are produced, the merits of each side are debated, and then the hypotheses are merged into a single, more accurate theory.
C . A topic is introduced, its known features and its mystery are discussed, and then future goals and applications are proposed.
D . A scientific enigma is explained, its history is chronicled, and then certain applications are attacked for their simplicity.
E . A point of view is presented, several hypotheses regarding the point of view materialize, and then the future of the point of view is predicted in the author's conclusion.

Passage A

The ceremony to name a child, formerly practiced among the Omaha and cognate tribes, took place in the spring. A tent was set apart and made sacred by the priest who had the hereditary right to perform the ceremony. As the occasion was one of tribal interest, many people flocked to the scene of the rite. A large stone was brought and placed on the east side of the fire that was burning in the center of the tent. All the mothers who had children of the proper age wended their way to this tent, each one leading her little child, who carried in its hands a new pair of moccasins. The mother and priest exchanged ritual greeting, and the child entered the tent with the priest. They went to the fire place and faced the East while the priest sang an invocation to the Four Winds.

During a ceremony with many ritual songs, the priest lifted the child by the arms so that its bare feet rested upon the stone, as it faced the South; then he repeated this for each of the other directions and put the new moccasins on the feet of the child. The priest then set the child on its feet and made it take four steps toward the East; these steps are typical of its now enter-ing into life. Then the priest led the child to the entrance of the tent, where he called aloud the tribal name of the child.

This ceremony, which is spoken of as "Turning the child," is highly symbolic. The Winds are the messengers of the great invisible Wakon'da and bring the breath of life and strength to man. All the children of the tribe passed through this ceremony and in this way received their sacred personal names, which were never dropped throughout their afterlife, not even when a man took a new name.

Passage B

The bestowal of a new name upon a Native American adult generally took place at some tribal ceremony when all the people

were gathered together. In this way as much publicity as
possible was given to the act.

Among the Pawnee tribe there were three requirements that had to be met in order to take a new name: a man could only take a new name after the performance of an act indicative of
ability or strength of character; the name had to be assumed openly in the presence of the people to whom the act it commemorated was known;
it was necessary that it should be announced in connection with a ritual ceremony, which consisted of a dramatic poem in three parts.

The first part gives briefly the institution of the rite of changing one's name in consequence of a new achievement; the second shows how the man was enabled to accomplish this act. It begins with his lonely vigil and fast when he cried to the powers for help; the scene then shifts to the circle of the lesser powers, who, in council, deliberate on his petition which makes its way to them and finally wins their consent; then the winds summon the messengers and these, gathering at the command of the lesser powers, are sent to earth to the man crying in lonely places, to grant him his desire. This part closes with a few vivid words which set forth that only by the favor of the powers had the man been able to do the deed. The third part deals with the man's names—the one to be discarded and the one now to be assumed.

Thus, it is indicated that a man's name stood for what he had shown himself to be by the light of his actions, that this was recognized by his tribesmen, and that it was proclaimed by one having charge of mediatory rites through which man can be approached by the supernatural.

19. Passage A supports which of the following contentions about the naming ceremony?
   A. The parents played an important role in the ceremony.
   B. There were three requirements for performing the ceremony.
   C. Undergoing the ceremony was voluntary.
   D. It was performed on an annual basis.
   E. The ceremony is still in use among some tribes today.

20. Both passages contain
   A. the requirements for undergoing the ceremony
   B. a detailed description of the ceremony performed
   C. symbolic meanings of the elements utilized
   D. a description of the actions of the priest during the ceremony
   E. a summary of the dramatic elements employed

21. The primary purpose of both passages is to
   A. advocate preservation of traditional rituals
   B. evaluate the artistic features of two procedures
   C. correct misinterpretations of a culture's practices
   D. analyze controversial customs among Native American tribes
   E. identify similar approaches to different issues

22. According to the information contained in both passages, all of the following symbolic elements play a role in naming ceremonies EXCEPT:

- A. fasting
- B. drinking
- C. cardinal directions
- D. fire
- E. wind

23. The third paragraph of Passage B serves primarily to
    - A. summarize the purpose and performance of a rite
    - B. expound upon a previously mentioned feature
    - C. provide interpretation of various symbolic elements
    - D. analyze an assertion in greater depth
    - E. proffer an example of cultural factors driving a practice

24. In Passage B, the phrase "mediatory rites" refers to
    - A. the role of the priest to speak between man and spirit
    - B. the transition from one name to another
    - C. the dramatic and symbolic nature of the ritual
    - D. the fact that the rite takes place in the middle stage of life
    - E. the belief in the intervention of supernatural beings

25. Based on the information in Passage B, which of the following men would most likely be allowed to take a new name?
    - A. a teenage boy undergoing his transition into manhood
    - B. a man who survived a near-fatal injury
    - C. a warrior who saved the life of a tribesman in battle
    - D. a man who successfully hunted a dangerous game animal
    - E. a tribe leader who negotiated a trade agreement with a nearby tribe

Section 4 Writing Sample

Johnson, Stevens, & Kunam, a mid-sized advertising firm, is seeking a new manager for one of its oldest accounts, a snack food company. Using the following facts, write an essay within the time limit of 35 minutes in which you argue for hiring one of the following applicants over the other based on these two criteria:

The firm wants to hire someone who knows how to appeal to the client's ideal demographic — young adults who are technologically savvy.

The firm wants to hire someone with a significant amount of advertising experience.

Tyler is a recent graduate of a well-recognized journalism program, where he majored in digital media. He interned for six months with a large advertising firm that specializes in innovative campaigns that emphasize reaching college-age adults through social media, cellphone applications, and other innovative technologies. The glowing recommendation letter written by his internship supervisor confirms that Tyler is proficient in new technologies and has impressed clients with his creativity and innovation.

Sofia has worked as an advertising account executive for more than 30 years. She has managed successful campaigns for a variety of products, including comestibles, but she admittedly has little experience with digital media and new technologies. Her impressive portfolio contains a plethora of award-winning examples of print and TV advertisements.

Test 2

Section 1 Analytical Reasoning

Time: 35 minutes for 25 questions

Directions: Each group of questions in this section is based on a set of conditions. In answering some of the questions, it may be useful to draw a rough diagram. Choose the response that most accurately and completely answers each question and blacken the corresponding space on your answer sheet.

Analytical Reasoning

Questions 1–5

A veterinarian will be using four large animal cages for transport: Cage 1, Cage 2, Cage 3, and Cage 4. Each cage has an upper berth and a lower berth, and each berth will be occupied by exactly one animal, either male or female. The following rules govern assignment of animals to cage berths:

Exactly three berths will contain males.

The upper berths of Cages 1 and 2 will contain females.

If a cage has a male in one of its berths, it will carry a female in the other.

If a male is assigned to the lower berth of Cage 3, then the upper berth of Cage 4 will contain a male.

F F F M
1 2 3 4
    M F

1. If a female is assigned to both berths of Cage 3, then which one of the following could be two other berths that also contain females?
   A. the upper berth of Cage 1 and the lower berth of Cage 2
   B. the lower berth of Cage 1 and the upper berth of Cage 4
   C. the lower berth of Cage 1 and the upper berth of Cage 2
   D. the upper berth of Cage 2 and the lower berth of Cage 4
   E. the lower berth of Cage 2 and the lower berth of Cage 4

2. It CANNOT be true that females are assigned to both
   A. the lower berth of Cage 1 and the lower berth of Cage 4
   B. the lower berth of Cage 1 and the lower berth of Cage 2
   C. the lower berth of Cage 1 and the upper berth of Cage 3
   D. the lower berth of Cage 2 and the lower berth of Cage 4
   E. the upper berth of Cage 3 and the lower berth of Cage 4

3. If the upper berth of Cage 4 contains a female, then a female must also be assigned to which one of the following berths?
   A. the lower berth of Cage 1
   B. the lower berth of Cage 4
   C. the lower berth of Cage 2
   D. the lower berth of Cage 3
   E. the upper berth of Cage 3

4. If a male is assigned to the lower berth of Cage 3, which one of the following is a complete and accurate list of the berths that CANNOT be assigned males?
   A. the upper berth of Cage 1, the upper berth of Cage 2
   B. the upper berth of Cage 1, the upper berth of Cage 2, the upper berth of Cage 3
   C. the upper berth of Cage 1, the upper berth of Cage 2, the lower berth of Cage 4
   D. the upper berth of Cage 1, the upper berth of Cage 2, the upper berth of Cage 3, the lower berth of Cage 4
   E. the upper berth of Cage 1, the lower berth of Cage 1, the upper berth of Cage 2, the upper berth of Cage 3, the lower berth of Cage 4

5. If the lower berth of Cage 2 contains a female, then it could be true that females are assigned to both
   A. the lower berth of Cage 1 and the upper berth of Cage 4
   B. the lower berth of Cage 1 and the lower berth of Cage 4
   C. the upper berth of Cage 3 and the upper berth of Cage 4
   D. the lower berth of Cage 3 and the lower berth of Cage 4
   E. the lower berth of Cage 3 and the upper berth of Cage 3

Questions 6–12 refer to the following scenario.

A ballroom dance club has seven members: four women — Madeleine, Mila, Olivia, and Avery — and three men — Henry, Jacob, and Charles. They have entered a ballroom competition that has five events performed in this order: foxtrot, paso doble, rumba, tango, and waltz. Each member of the club competes in exactly one event. They compete either in pairs of one man and one woman or as solo performers. The following rules determine who dances with whom and in which event:

Henry competes as a solo performer.
Mila competes as part of a pair.
Olivia competes in the rumba.
Jacob cannot compete in an event immediately before or immediately after the event in which Charles competes.

6. If Avery is the only member who competes in the foxtrot, and Jacob competes in the rumba, then which one of the following must be true?

   A . Henry competes in the paso doble.
   B . Henry competes in the waltz.
   C . Madeleine competes in the paso doble.
   D . Mila competes in the tango.
   E . Mila competes in the waltz.

7. If Henry chooses his event first, what is the maximum number of the remaining events from which Mila can choose her own event?

   A . one
   B . two
   C . three
   D . four
   E . five

8. If solo women compete in the foxtrot and the paso doble, then which of the following members must compete in the tango?

   A . Henry
   B . Madeleine
   C . Mila
   D . Mila and Charles
   E . Avery and Jacob

9. Which one of the following is a complete and accurate list of the members who CANNOT dance solo?

   A . Jacob, Mila, and Avery
   B . Charles, Jacob, and Mila
   C . Madeleine and Mila
   D . Madeleine, Mila, and Avery
   E . Mila and Olivia

10. Which of the following is a complete and accurate list of the women who could compete solo?

    A . Madeleine
    B . Avery
    C . Madeleine and Olivia
    D . Madeleine and Avery
    E . Madeleine, Olivia, and Avery

11. If the four women compete in four consecutive events, and Mila competes in the waltz, then which of the following is a complete and accurate list of the events in which members must compete as solo performers?

    A . foxtrot and paso doble
    B . foxtrot and tango
    C . paso doble
    D . foxtrot, paso doble, rumba, and tango
    E . tango

12. If the three men compete in the first three events, then which one of the following must be true?

    A . Jacob competes in the foxtrot.
    B . Jacob and Madeleine compete in the same event.
    C . Jacob and Mila compete in the same event.
    D . Charles competes in the rumba.
    E . Mila competes in the foxtrot.

Questions 13 - 19

Eight players—A, B, C, D, E, F, G, and H—come to a soccer game and split into two teams. Four people are on team 1, and four people are on team 2. Their grouping is governed by the following constraints:

If A is on team 1, then B is on team 2.
If D is on team 1, then F is on team 2.
If B is on team 2, then D is on team 1.
E is not on a team with F.

13. Which of the following is a group that could comprise team 1?
    A. A, D, F, G
    B. E, G, H, C
    C. H, C, G, D
    D. G, D, E, A
    E. A, D, B, E

14. If B is on team 2 with A, then which of the following could be true?
    A. E is on team 2.
    B. A is on team 1.
    C. C is on team 1.
    D. D is on team 2.
    E. G, H, and C are all on the same team.

15. If A and F are on the same team, then which of the following must be true?
    A. E is on team 1.
    B. B is on team 2.
    C. C is on team 1.
    D. D is not on a team.
    E. F is on the same team as H.

16. If D and B are on the same team, then which of the following must be true?
    A. C shares a team with G.
    B. G shares a team with E.
    C. B shares a team with F.
    D. D shares a team with H.
    E. A shares a team with F.

17. Which of the following people can never be on the same team as F?
    A. A
    B. B
    C. C
    D. D
    E. E

18. If F is on team 1, then how many different configurations are possible for the people on the teams?
    A. one
    B. two
    C. three
    D. four
    E. five

If D and A are on separate teams, then which of the following must NOT be true?
    A. E is on team 2.
    B. B is on team 1.
    C. G is on team 2 with H.
    D. B is on team 2.
    E. D is on team 1.

Questions 20 – 25

A live music gig features five bands—the Rollers, the Rockers, the Hollie Bush Boys, the Novas, and the Truckers—that will sing ten songs.

Each band performs exactly two of the songs: One band performs songs 1 and 6, one band performs songs 2 and 7, one band performs songs 3 and 8, one band performs songs 4 and 9, and one band performs songs 5 and 10. The following conditions apply:

Neither of the Rockers' songs is performed immediately before either of the Hollie Bush Boys's.

The Rollers do not sing the ninth song.

The Truckers' first song is after (but not necessarily immediately after) the Novas' first song.

At least one of the Rollers' songs is immediately after one of the Truckers' songs.

19. Which one of the following could be an accurate list of the bands performing the first five songs, in order from song 1 to song 5?
    A. Rollers, Rockers, Novas, Hollie Bush Boys, Truckers

- B. Rockers, Novas, Truckers, Rollers, Hollie Bush Boys
- C. Hollie Bush Boys, Novas, Rollers, Rockers, Truckers
- D. Truckers, Rockers, Novas, Hollie Bush Boys, Rollers
- E. Novas, Truckers, Rollers, Rockers, Hollie Bush Boys

20. If the Rollers sing the eighth song, then for exactly how many of the ten songs can one determine which band sings the song?
    - A. ten
    - B. eight
    - C. six
    - D. four
    - E. two

21. If the Truckers sing the fourth song, then which one of the
following could be true?
    - A. The Rollers sing song 1.
    - B. The Rollers sing song 3.
    - C. The Rockers sing song 5.
    - D. The Hollie Bush Boys sing song 3.
    - E. The Novas sing song 5.

22. Which one of the following could be true?
    - A. The Rollers sing song 4.
    - B. The Rockers sing song 5.
    - C. The Hollie Bush Boys sing song 5.
    - D. The Novas sing song 10.
    - E. The Truckers sing song 6.

23. The Rollers CANNOT perform which one of the following songs?
    - A. song 1
    - B. song 2
    - C. song 3
    - D. song 6
    - E. song 10

24. Which one of the following could be an accurate list of the bands performing the last five songs, in order from song 6 to song 10?
    - A. Rollers, Novas, Rockers, Truckers, Hollie Bush Boys
    - B. Rockers, Hollie Bush Boys, Novas, Truckers, Rollers
    - C. Hollie Bush Boys, Rockers, Novas, Truckers, Rollers
    - D. Novas, Rockers, Truckers, Rollers, Hollie Bush Boys
    - E. Truckers, Rollers, Rockers, Novas, Hollie Bush Boys

Section 2 Logical Reasoning

Time: 35 minutes for 24 questions

Directions: Read the passage and choose the best answer. Some questions may have more than one answer that looks right. Select the one that answers the question most completely. Don't assume anything that isn't directly stated, and don't let your imagination run wild; all the information you need is in the arguments and the answer choices.

1. Consumer review: This mail-order catalog claims that its customers save money by buying clothing through it, but the economy it promises is illusory because it only occasionally marks down its normal prices. Which one of the following is an assumption on which the consumer review's argument depends?
    A . This catalog's competitors mark down their normal prices more frequently and by greater amounts.
    B . This catalog is economical only when its normal prices are marked down more than occasionally.
    C . This catalog marks its normal prices down by smaller amounts than do its competitors.
    D . The competitors have lower normal prices.
    E . Consumers should make purchases by mail order only when the normal prices are marked down.

2. The archaeological findings at level IV a of a bronze-age settlement in Greece show how the settlement met its end. The village was surrounded by a thick, defensive wall. The findings include a large number of clay vessels sunk in the ground, as though for long-term storage of food during a siege. A number of bronze arrowheads were found, and at least one of the structures seems to have suffered a fire. Therefore, this settlement was clearly destroyed in war, either with its neighbors or with foreign invaders. Which one of the following most accurately describes a flaw in the argument?
    A . The argument is circular, with the premises taking for granted the truth of the conclusion.
    B . The evidence is varied, but the conclusion is unified and therefore suspect.
    C . The argument depends on intermediate conclusions, which make the final conclusion invalid.
    D . The argument makes a historical conclusion but does not give specific dates to support it.
    E . None of the pieces of evidence point directly to the conclusion, and all of them could lead to different conclusions.

3. Oceanographer:The size of oceanic waves is a function of the velocity of the wind and of fetch, the length of the surface of the water subject to those winds. The impact of waves against a coastline is a function of the size of the waves and the shape of the sea bottom. The degree of erosion to which a coastline is subject is a function of the average impact of

waves and the geologic composition of the coastline. If the oceanographer's statements are true, which one of the following must also be true?

    A. The fetch of winds is related to the shape of the sea bottom.
    B. The size of oceanic waves will not fluctuate far from an average for any given stretch of ocean.
    C. The degree of erosion to which a coastline is subject is related to the shape of the sea bottom.
    D. The size of oceanic waves is related to the shape of the sea bottom.
    E. The average velocity of the wind in an area plays no role in the degree of erosion to which a coastline is subject.

4. Historian: For a historian to assert that one historical event or circumstance caused another is nearly impossible. Given any coherent historical narrative, the sequence of events makes the notion of causation a tempting trap; a subsequent event can seem a necessary outcome of those that preceded it. But this is a mere consequence of the backward-looking perspective of the historian's art. That one event did in fact happen, and that other events did in fact happen prior to it does not make the subsequent event inevitable or a direct outcome of those that went before. The claim that "this is a mere consequence of the backward-looking perspective of the historian's art" plays which one of the following roles in the historian's argument?

    A. It is used to identify the theoretical imperative that is the argument's concern.
    B. It is an illustration of a premise that is used to support the argument's conclusion.
    C. It is used to indirectly support a claim that the argument in turn uses to directly support the conclusion.
    D. It is used to explain a consideration that may be taken to undermine the argument's conclusion.
    E. It is the conclusion that the argument aims to support.

5. Despite five consecutive years in which global consumption of grain has been greater than global production, it is unlikely that the world is facing a near-term crisis in the food supply. The average shortfalls have been mainly due to reduced output from farms in China, which is moving from a policy of central control over agricultural production to a more market-driven model. Therefore, if demand for grain continues to fall short of supply, Chinese production of grain should increase dramatically. Which one of the following principles most helps to justify this reasoning?

    A. Global markets respond more slowly than regional markets, so local rates of production usually change more rapidly than the global average.
    B. When agricultural production is centrally controlled, it is unable to respond to changing demand by adjusting rates of supply.
    C. Average shortfalls are most readily remedied by local increases in production.
    D. When agricultural production is market-driven, it is likely to respond to rising demand by increasing production.

E. Centrally controlled agricultural production has been shown to be more inefficient than market-driven models.

6. Economist: Health insurers are largely immune to the factors that are limiting profit in many sectors of the healthcare economy. Consumers have shown a willingness to pay almost any price for health insurance premiums. Capital demands, which are the responsibility of doctors and hospitals, are increasing dramatically, even as cost-containment measures, largely encouraged by the insurers and their friends in government, have forced new levels of fiscal discipline upon hospitals and doctors. Patients still need MRIs and buildings to put them in, but hospitals are limited in how much they can charge patients for the use of these facilities. Which one of the following most accurately describes the role that the statement "patients still need MRIs and buildings to put them in" plays in the economist's argument?

A. It is a specific example of a general condition described in the course of the argument.
B. It is used to counter a consideration that may be taken to undermine the argument.
C. It is used to indirectly support the claim made by the argument.
D. It describes a social side effect of the benefit with which the argument is concerned.
E. It introduces the conclusion that the argument intends to support.

7. As peer-to-peer (PTP) file-sharing networks flourished, the ability of consumers to download music without paying seriously damaged the prosperity of the recording industry. The numbers speak for themselves. During this time, revenues from sales of CDs in the United States fell by tens of millions of dollars a year, despite the fact that prices for individual CDs kept pace with inflation. Clearly, then, PTP file-sharing was killing the recording industry. The argument depends on assuming which one of the following?

A. that all sharing from PTP networks violates copyright
B. that no other explanations exist for the decreasing revenues from CD sales
C. that the musicians and producers have a right to profit from the distribution of music
D. that people who download music would otherwise have purchased it on CD
E. that a complex relationship exists between file-sharing and the market in music, both online and on CD

8. Engineer: In any complex machine on which human life depends, critical systems must have many layers of built-in redundancy. So in designing airplanes, whose control surfaces depend on hydraulic systems for their movement, engineers must include multiple independent redundant systems of hydraulic lines, each capable of giving the pilot control of the airplane's control surfaces. More redundancy is always better than less, so if an airplane design is deemed relatively safe with three redundant hydraulic systems, it must be deemed safer with four, and safer still with five. The engineer's argument is most vulnerable to criticism on the grounds that it

A. assumes that redundant systems will not be subject to simultaneous failure
B. fails to take into account any practical factors that may limit the number of

redundant systems or practical trade-offs involved in increasing levels of redundancy

C. focuses on one area — movement of the control surfaces — without taking into account other important considerations of safety

D. is limited to a single kind of engineering project and may not be applicable as a general rule

E. gives no comprehensive criteria for judging relative levels of safety, according to which you could evaluate its claim that increasing redundancy yields increasing safety

9. Forcing businesses to furnish employees with paid leave for family concerns, such as paternity leave or leave to care for a sick child, is a terrible idea. If a business allows employees to take this time off, the workers will take advantage of the privilege and come to work as little as possible. This will destroy productivity and workplace morale.

9. Which one of the following, if true, most seriously weakens the argument?

A. European countries guarantee employees generous family leave and paid vacation time, but the European standard of living is slightly below that of the United States.

B. Most male workers refuse to take paternity leave even though it is allowed under federal law and their employers encourage it; they fear they may anger co-workers and harm their chances for promotion if they take time off for what is still seen as a frivolous reason.

C. The FMLA requires employers to grant employees 12 weeks a year of unpaid leave for family purposes; although employers save money because the leave is unpaid, they often must spend money to find a replacement for the employee who takes time off.

D. In some workplaces, the loss of a single employee at a busy time of year can be devastating, even if that employee plans to return after a few weeks; allowing family leave can overwhelm the employees who stay on the job.

E. Allowing employees to take leave for family matters reduces absenteeism, improves morale, and surprisingly increases productivity because the employees who are granted leave tend to work much harder and more efficiently when they come back to work.

10. Casino gambling tends to be detrimental to individuals who live in the county where the casino is located, but paradoxically, it benefits businesses in those same counties. Individual bankruptcy rates in counties with casinos are more than double the national average. Bankruptcy rates for businesses in the same counties are 35 percent lower than the national average. Which one of the following, if true, most helps to explain this apparent paradox?

A. Businesses profit from casino gambling because they take in money from local and visiting gamblers, whereas local individuals have more opportunities to lose money gambling.

B. Casinos are known to take advantage of gamblers by setting odds in such a way that the casino always makes a profit.

C. Counties with casinos have many business opportunities for entrepreneurs who want to open hotels, restaurants, and other service businesses.

D. Gambling functions as an addictive disease in many people; they find themselves unable to stop gambling even when they're seriously in debt and must borrow money to continue.

E. Counties that vote to allow casinos to open generally are poor counties with high unemployment and low levels of education.

11. Social services worker: We approve of the government's new policy on food stamps. Instead of issuing actual stamps, the government now provides recipients with debit cards that they can use to buy groceries. Each month their accounts are electronically credited with their allowance, and they can spend the money just as if it were in a bank account but only on specific approved items. This method eliminates the inconvenience and embarrassment associated with food stamps, increases the number of qualified recipients who actually buy food with their allowance, and prevents the type of fraud that was a problem associated with the paper coupons. All of the following, if true, help to support the position of the social services worker EXCEPT:

A. In communities that use the food stamp debit cards, participation in food stamp programs has increased 74 percent since changing to cards from coupons.

B. Paper food stamp coupons have long been abused by people who trade them for drugs or weapons at several cents on the dollar.

C. The food stamp program is meant to improve nutrition among people with low incomes, and the government has long wanted to make sure program funds are used to buy food.

D. People used to have to pick up their paper coupons at a government office once a month, which proved too inconvenient for many people who lacked transportation or free time.

E. Some food stamp recipients say they prefer the paper coupons because they can't tell how much money they have in their debit card accounts.

12. Primatologist: We have discovered a new kind of primate in Madagascar, the fat-tailed lemur. These lemurs hibernate, sleeping in holes in trees for up to seven months out of the year. Winter temperatures in Madagascar rarely drop below 86 degrees, so these lemurs do not hibernate to escape the cold but perhaps to conserve energy during the dry season, when food is scarce. This is the first time anyone has found an animal that hibernates during hot weather, disproving the common belief that only animals in cold climates hibernate. Which one of the following most accurately describes the role played in the primatologist's argument by the assertion that this is the first time anyone has found an animal that hibernates during hot weather?

A. It challenges the long-held belief that primates never hibernate.

B. It accuses scientists who have studied hibernation in the past of wrongfully assuming that hibernation only occurs in cold weather.

C. It highlights the importance of this discovery because it disproves a long-held theory about hibernation.

D. It calls into question the assumption that this behavior is true hibernation

and suggests that it may be something else.
   E. It sets up a rival theory so that the primatologist can disprove it.

13. Director: I've decided to cast the famous American actor Burt Lancaster as the prince in my epic film of the Sicilian classic novel The Leopard. I want him for his star appeal and his massive dignity. The film will be in Italian, but Lancaster can't speak Italian, so I'll let him speak his lines in English and then have an Italian actor dub them in Italian. The result will be a seamless Italian film with a famous actor to help sales. Which one of the following is an assumption on which the director's argument depends?
   A. Italian audiences will refuse to see a film of an Italian classic that does not use an Italian actor in the title role.
   B. The other actors in the film may object to playing their scenes with a character who cannot speak their language.
   C. To increase sales, having a famous actor in the title role of a film is more important than having an actor who can speak the film's language.
   D. Teaching Lancaster enough Italian to allow him to deliver his lines in the correct language would be impossible.
   E. Lancaster would feel uncomfortable working with a director and crew who did not speak English.

14. George: We should eradicate mosquitoes from the earth. Mosquitoes cause a great deal of harm to humans, transmitting serious diseases such as malaria, dengue fever, and encephalitis, and they don't do anything desirable. Ecologists have found that the loss of a single species from an ecosystem doesn't usually harm the rest of the ecosystem, so eradicating mosquitoes wouldn't harm the environment, which of course would be undesirable. Which one of the following, if true, would most weaken George's argument?
   A. Mosquito-borne diseases such as malaria are responsible for millions of deaths and millions of dollars of lost productivity every year.
   B. One inevitable consequence of restoring wetlands to their original state is an increase in mosquito populations.
   C. Mosquitoes have historically kept human and other animal populations down by spreading disease among them.
   D. Many animals eat mosquitoes and other flying insects.
   E. The only substances that could eradicate all mosquitoes would also kill off many birds and beneficial insects.

15. Public parks are intended for use by all citizens equally. But when groups such as schools or churches use a park for parties or other organized events, they bring large numbers of people to the park at one time. Therefore, there should be strict rules against large groups using public parks. The argument's reasoning is vulnerable to criticism on the grounds that the argument takes for granted that
   A. large groups of people may be noisy or become violent
   B. individuals have complained about large groups of people using public parks
   C. public parks are designed with use by organized groups in mind
   D. members of organized groups, like other individuals, pay taxes that support public parks

E. large numbers of people coming to a park prevent individuals from enjoying use of the park

16. Employers have recently begun to offer their employees the opportunity to save money for future healthcare or family care expenses in flexible spending accounts, or FSAs. These accounts allow employees to set aside pretax salary income for specific expenses, which can result in a substantial savings on income tax. Surprisingly, though, very few employees have taken advantage of FSAs. Which one of the following, if true, contributes most to an explanation of why few employees have chosen to save money in FSAs?

- A. Insurance companies have started to offer employees debit cards to go with FSAs, which makes it much easier to spend FSA funds.
- B. Not all employers offer FSAs to their employees.
- C. Employees can use funds saved in FSAs to pay for over-the-counter drugs and other healthcare costs that are not covered by insurance.
- D. Funds saved in FSAs must be spent during the plan year or forfeited.
- E. Employers who move to consumer-driven healthcare plans with high deductibles are finding that more of their employees choose to open FSAs.

17. Many Latin American countries established democratic governments in the past decade. Recently, however, six elected heads of state have been ousted during violent revolutions. A majority of people in those countries, dissatisfied with continuing poverty, have stated that they would install a dictator if he promised to improve economic conditions. These statements, if true, most strongly support which one of the following conclusions?

- A. Some 220 million Latin Americans, nearly half the population of the region, live in grinding poverty without many of the basic necessities of life.
- B. The governments of these six Latin American countries, though democratically elected, are plagued by corruption and graft.
- C. A majority of residents of these six Latin American countries do not believe that democracy is necessarily the best form of government for them.
- D. Weak governments in Latin America are one of the reasons drug trafficking and illegal immigration to the United States have increased in the last decade.
- E. Some citizens of Latin American countries have expressed the opinion that rule by organized crime is preferable to democratically elected leadership.

18. Years ago people enjoyed homemade eggnog and cookie dough made with raw eggs without fear, but today raw eggs are spoken of as a biohazard, a potential hotbed of salmonella waiting to cause disease and death with the slightest contact. In previous decades, salmonella was generally found on the outside of eggshells, mainly from the eggs having come in contact with the waste products of the chickens who laid them. More recently, however, a growing number of chickens are themselves infected with salmonella, thus allowing the bacterium to be present inside the egg itself. So where once simply washing uncracked eggs protected diners from illness — usually some form of

gastrointestinal distress, only rarely fatal — now only cooking eggs thoroughly can guarantee a safe dining experience. Which one of the following most accurately expresses the main conclusion of the argument?

A. Salmonella poisoning is on the increase but is rarely fatal.

B. The relationship between salmonella and eggs has in fact changed over the years, justifying the recent caution with which people regard raw eggs.

C. Some caution is merited when handling raw eggs, although the facts behind salmonella and eggs do not merit extreme levels of caution.

D. The risk of food poisoning from eating raw eggs is related to the conditions under which the eggs are produced, which have changed over time.

E. The caution with which people regard their food is related to a better understanding of the science behind food poisoning.

19. Software engineers know that a poorly written application can consume more memory than it should and that running out of memory can cause an application to crash. However, if a crashing application causes the whole operating system to crash, the fault lies with the operating system. Which one of the following, if true, is least helpful in establishing that this conclusion is properly drawn?

A. Operating systems with generous amounts of memory are less susceptible to crashing, even when applications are poorly written.

B. Operating systems can isolate the memory used by individual applications, even when an application uses a large amount of memory.

C. An operating system can monitor an application's consumption of memory and take action when that gets too high.

D. Techniques for programming operating systems to catch and handle memory errors are well-defined and well-known among programmers.

E. Because many applications can run simultaneously under a single operating system, the operating system should have a well-defined method of managing memory consumption.

20. The document was published under a license that allows others to copy it and disseminate it as long as they do so for noncommercial purposes only. Company A included copies of the document in a training manual that it marketed and sold, arguing that the license was invalid. However, even if the license were proved invalid, the copyright was still valid, leaving Company A with no rights to use the document in any way at all. Which one of the following situations best demonstrates the principle illustrated by this argument?

A. The warranty on the laptop computer claimed to be rendered void if the user opened the case. But the manual that came with the laptop included instructions for opening the case to upgrade the computer's memory. Consumers successfully argued that those instructions constituted an endorsement of users' opening the case and that, therefore, the warranty was not void.

B. When the 13-year-olds were caught trying to enter an NC-17 movie at a multiplex, they argued that the cashier at the ticket counter had sold them tickets for that movie. The manager explained that the cashier's error did not change the rules of age limits and movie ratings.

C. A restaurant was fined by the Alcoholic Beverage Commission for serving distilled liquors when its license covered only tool and wine. The restaurant's manager argued that he had applied for the proper license and expected to receive it within days. The ABC countered that a license was valid only from the moment the restaurant posted it on the premises.

D. Ted's parents have stated that he cannot drive the station wagon unless it is to Alice's house. When his mother saw the station wagon parked at the mall, some miles away, Ted argued that Alice was not at home. Ted's mom pointed out that he ought, upon discovering that fact, to have driven straight home.

E. The celebrity sued the magazine for publishing photographs of him sunning himself in his backyard, which was enclosed by a high fence. The magazine claimed that he was a public figure and did, therefore, have the same rights to privacy as normal citizens. The celebrity claimed that the extensive fence around his yard justified his privacy rights when behind it, despite his prominent stature in the eyes of the public.

21. Scholar: Greek epic poetry emerged as an art form before any of it was ever written down. Singers developed a specialized vocabulary that allowed them to compose poems about the heroes of the Trojan War as they sang them. These poems were neither made up from scratch as the singer sang nor fixed texts that were memorized and repeated verbatim. Even after written texts were created that captured these orally composed poems, the tradition continued to evolve, with written texts of the same poem differing from place to place and from time to time, according to the circumstances of their production and the interests of their creators and their intended audiences. If the scholar's statements are true, which one of the following must be true?

A. Each written edition derived from the first written version of an orally composed epic.

B. No single written edition of a Greek epic can claim to represent the "original" version.

C. The poems inevitably grew longer and more narratologically complex over the centuries.

D. The tradition of composing epics orally died away as the poems came to be written down.

E. The older editions of the poems were less likely to have been influenced by local politics than subsequent editions.

22. Curator: This museum does not grant people the right to use images of items in its collection in online publications. We are obliged to do everything in our power to ensure the continued appeal of visiting our collection in person. The curator's argument depends on assuming which one of the following?

A. Taking photographs of art objects, especially using a flash, can damage the objects by accelerating the fading of paint.

- B. The museum sells pictures of its collection in its gift shop, which is an important source of income for the museum.
- C. Images placed online are easily copied and reused by other people.
- D. The quality of most electronic images, especially those online, falls short of the professional standards of the museum.
- E. If people see online images of items in the museum's collection, they will no longer be interested in seeing the collection with their own eyes.

23. Career counselor: Many large international companies have changed their practices regarding international assignments. They are placing much more emphasis on helping spouses of expatriate employees to adjust to the foreign environment. This has reduced premature returns by 67 percent. Which one of the following is an assumption upon which the career counselor's argument depends?

- A. Spousal and marital difficulties were formerly responsible for a large number of premature returns from foreign assignments.
- B. When an employee is placed in a foreign assignment for a year or less, his or her family sees the assignment as an adventure.
- C. Expatriate employees work long hours and travel a great deal, and their children make new friends at school, but spouses often have no friends and no work to support them while they're abroad.
- D. The majority of international assignments today last for less than a year, but ten years ago, 70 percent of them lasted much longer than one year.
- E. Many companies now offer expatriate spouses language training, career guidance, and assistance in finding homes and schools.

24. Traveler: When I flew to Boston on Tuesday, I checked my suitcase but carried my computer on the plane. When I arrived at Logan Airport, none of the checked bags from the flight had arrived. The baggage office clerk was very helpful with my polite questions but punished the other passengers who were so rude by making them wait for her assistance. Which one of the following principles is best illustrated by the traveler's reasoning?

- A. A stitch in time saves nine.
- B. Do not price an unborn calf.
- C. Do not put all your eggs in one basket.
- D. Neither a borrower nor a lender be.
- E. You catch more flies with honey than you do with vinegar.

Section 3 Reading Comprehension

Time: 35 minutes for 26 questions

Directions: Read each passage and answer the questions that follow it. Some questions may have more than one answer that looks correct. In that case, pick the one that answers the question most completely and correctly. Don't assume anything that isn't stated in the passage or the questions. All the information you need to answer the questions is contained in the passage, questions, and answer choices.

Questions 1–6 refer to the following passage.

Black Apollo, by Kenneth Mannin, describes the life of Ernest Everett Just, one of the first bkack scientists in America. Manning recounts Just's impoverished origins in South Carolina, his adaptations to a white educational system, and hiss careers as a zoology professor at Howard University and as a an embryologist at Marine Biological Laboratory. Despite countless difficulties imposed upon him by a world in which a black person was not supposed to practice science. Just became an internationally esteemed biologist. His story is one of courage determination. and dedication to science But Manning's goals are more far-reaching than to simply tell a story or describe one man's life. Alter all, though Just was a brilliant biologist. he

was not ultimately pivotal to the development of either science or rage relations in the 20th century. The' Issues brought out in his story however, are pivotal. A comprehensive appreciation of the conditions that Just faced in his daily work offers a powerful lens through which to examine the development of science and racial boundaries in America.

Manning wrote Just's story as a biography. In some respects, biography does not seem to be a promising medium for great historical work. Biographies simply tell a story. Most students receive their introductions to history in science in the worship full biographies of past scientific giants. Benjamin Franklin and Albert Einstein offer excellent examples to young students of how scientists contribute to society. Biographies are popular for children's reading lists (and bestseller lists) because they have simple subjects, can present clear moral statements and manage to teach a little history ant the same time. This simplicity of form, however does not preclude the biography from being a powerful medium of historical work and social commentary.

The biography yields particular rewards for the historian of science, indeed a central reason for the discipline is to show that science is a product of social forces. This principle implies that historians and sociologists have insights on the practice of science that scientists to whom the subject would otherwise fall, are less likely to produce. Moreover, if society does influence science, then it behoves historians to explain how such an important process works. The human orientation of the biography makes it an excellent medium in which historians can do this work. Were a researcher to investigate the development of scientific theory solely by reading the accounts written of a laboratory's experiments, by looking only at the science – the researcher would likely see a science moved by apparently rational forces toward a discernible goal. But this picture is incomplete and artificial. If that researcher examines a science the through people who generated it, a richer mosaic of actors emerges. The science biography has the potential to reveal both the person through the science and the science through the person. From these perspectives, the forces of politics, emotions and economics, each of which can direct science as much as rational thought, are more easily brought to light. Black Apollo is a riveting example of what a historian can accomplish with a skilful and directed use of biography.

1. Which one of the following most accurately states the main point of the passage?
   A. Ernest Everett Just was an extremely important biologist during the 20th century, both because of his contributions to the field of embryology and because of his race.
   B. Scientists tend to ignore the social, historical, and political forces that surround all scientific research and discovery, which makes their interpretations of scientific events incomplete.
   C. Biographies are a popular genre for children's books because they can tell discrete stories in an accessible fashion, incorporating scientific knowledge into a person's life and thereby making it more interesting to readers.
   D. Manning's work exemplifies how biography can be a powerful tool for a historian of science, who can use the genre to explore the effects of politics, economics, and emotions on the direction of scientific development.
   E. Kenneth Manning wrote Black Apollo to criticize racial prejudices and to prove that Ernest Everett Just could have been much more successful if he had not been the victim of discrimination.

2. According to the passage, the main goal of the discipline called history of science is to
   A. illuminate the effects of social forces on scientists in a way that scientists themselves are unlikely to do
   B. explain scientific discoveries in a manner that is easily understood by non-scientists
   C. write biographies of important scientific figures that portray their work against a social and political background
   D. influence scientific research by identifying the most important scientific contributions in history

E. provide an academic discipline that allows people without science training to study scientific concepts

3. What is the primary purpose of the second paragraph?

A. to describe the many things Ernest Everett Just accomplished despite the racial prejudice he faced
B. to suggest that biography is really too simple a historical form for the historian of science to use to convey complex ideas
C. to explain why biography is both a popular historical genre and a powerful medium for explaining the significance of scientific discoveries
D. to argue against using biographies to teach children about scientific figures from the past
E. to advocate increased teaching of the sciences in schools and universities

4. The author of the passage would be most likely to agree with which one of the following statements?

A. One of the best ways to come to an understanding of the realities of race relations and scientific development in the 20th century is to read an in-depth account of the life of one of the people who lived and worked in that world.
B. The goal of a historian of science is to glorify the accomplishments of his historical subjects, embellishing them if need be.
C. A scientific historian should pay close attention to the social and literary aspects of a scientific biography and play down the actual science, because readers can turn to scientific reports to get that information.
D. Ernest Everett Just was likely the most important black biologist, and in fact one of the most important biologists, of the 20th century.
E. Biography is too limited a genre to allow a historian of science to do justice to a topic, but it is useful occasionally because most readers find biographies more accessible than other historical formats.

5. According to the passage, why is Ernest Everett Just significant enough to warrant a biography?

A. Just was one of the first professional black scientists in the United States.
B. Just grew up in poverty but overcame this initial adversity to attend Howard University and then become a professional scientist.
C. Just was a biologist whose work was known and respected internationally.
D. Just's daily experiences illuminate the conditions characterized by both scientific research and racial relations during his lifetime.
E. Just became a college professor and an embryologist at Marine Biological Laboratory.

6. What does the author mean by the phrase "simplicity of form" (Line 38)?

A. the simple language used by many biographical writers
B. the easy-to-read page design used by most publishers of biographies
C. a writing style that is easy for schoolchildren to read and understand
D. the powerful social commentary that a heroic life story can contain

E. the straightforward organization of a biography, which follows the course of the subject's life

Questions 7–13 refer to the following passage.

Sodium lauryl sulfate (SLS) us an emulsifier and surfactant that produces lather and foam that can dissolve oil and dirt on skin and hair. SLS and another similar detergent, sodium laureth sulfate (SLES, are commonly used as foaming agents in cleaners, shampoos, and toothpaste. Both of these substances are derived from coconut oil. They make liquid and paste cleansers more effective at cleansing because they allow the cleanser to disperse more readily over the object being cleaned and make it easier to rinse the cleanser away. SLS and SLES have been used for years in numerous products sold to consumers. Other foaming agents are available, SLS and SLES have remained popular because of their low cost, effectiveness, lack of taste and odor and long history of safe use.

The use of SLs and SLES comes with a few minor risks. The substances burn human eyes, a phenomenon well known to anyone who has ever gotten a drop of shampoo in her eye. A high enough concentration of SLS will burn skin if it remains in contact with the skin for a long time, though normally this is not a problem because the products containing SLES or SLS are diluted with water and quickly washed away. SLS in toothpaste can cause diarrhea in someone who swallows a large quantity of it, but it is not known to be toxic if ingested in small quantities.

Many people have become afraid of SLS and SLES in recent years, largely as a result of widespread rumors circulated on the internet that blame SLS and SLES for causing numerous ailments in humans, including hair loss, dry skin, liver and kidney disease, blindness in children and cancer, SLS has been called one the most dangerous substances used in cosmetic products. Rumors wasn't that SLS and SLES can react with other ingredients in products to form nitrates which are potential carcinogens.

Detractors of SLS and SLES point out that these substances are used in cleansers intended for the floors of garages and bathrooms and in engine degreasers. This is true; it is also true that household and garbage cleaners are not sold for cosmetic use, come with warnings of possible skin and eye irritation and are perfectly safe to use for their intended purposes.

These internet warning of the dangers of SLS and SLES are absurd and unsubstantiated. The US food and drug administration (FDA) has approved the use of SLS and SLES in a number of personal care products. The Occupational Safety and Health Administration (OSHA), the International Agency for research on cancer, and the American Cancer Society have all done extensive research on SLS and SLES and concluded that they do not cause cancer.

7. Which one of the following best summarizes the main idea of the passage?

A. A few minor risks are associated with the use of SLS and SLES, but consumers should feel safe in using products containing these substances because the

FDA has approved them for use in personal care products.

B. Manufacturers of shampoos and toothpastes include the artificial chemicals SLS and SLES in their products because they are cheap and effective surfactants, despite the known dangers associated with them.

C. SLS and SLES are detergents that are commonly used in personal care products because they are effective and safe, despite unsubstantiated rumors to the contrary.

D. Widespread rumors circulated on the Internet blame SLS and SLES for numerous ailments in humans, including hair loss, dry skin, liver and kidney disease, blindness in children, and cancer.

E. It is entirely possible to use SLS and SLES in both personal care products such as shampoos and industrial products such as engine degreasers because, at lower concentrations, the substances are perfectly safe to use on human skin.

8. According to the passage, what are some of the household products that commonly contain SLS or SLES?

A. shampoo, mouthwash, sunscreen, and hair dye

B. shampoo, toothpaste, bathroom cleaners, and engine degreasers

C. toothpaste, engine degreasers, engine lubricants, and garage cleaners

D. mouthwash, facial moisturizers, and baby wipes

E. bathroom and kitchen cleaners, laundry detergents, and fabric softeners

9. The author mentions the FDA in the last paragraph most likely to

A. point out that the FDA has approved the use of SLS and SLES in personal care products

B. suggest that the FDA has the best interests of consumers at heart

C. imply that the FDA's opinion that SLS and SLES are safe for use in personal care products excuses manufacturers from testing their personal care products for safety

D. protest the FDA's approval of the use of SLS
and SLES in personal care products

E. refute claims that SLS and SLES are dangerous

10. According to the passage, what are some of the widely accepted risks of SLS exposure?

A. cancer, blindness, cataracts, dry skin, and diarrhea

B. burning eyes, burned skin after long exposure, liver disease, and kidney disease

C. skin irritation, eye irritation, hair loss, and diarrhea if ingested in large quantities

D. burning eyes, burned skin after long exposure, and diarrhea if ingested in large quantities

E. diarrhea, skin irritation after extended exposure, eye irritation, cataracts, and bladder cancer

11. Which one of the following best describes the organization of the passage?

A. a list of known risks of exposure to SLS and SLES; a list of unsubstantiated risks of exposure to SLS and SLES; a conclusion stating that SLS and SLES are perfectly safe

B. a description of several common surfactants and the way in which they work; several anecdotal accounts of injuries and illnesses allegedly caused by SLS and SLES; a call for the government to ban the use of SLS and SLES in consumer care products

C. a description of the chemical composition of SLS and SLES; a list of evidence against the use of SLS and SLES in personal care products; a proposal to manufacturers suggesting that they use only naturally occurring substances in their products

D. an overview of the many uses of SLS and SLES; an explanation of why manufacturers use these substances in both consumer care and household cleaning products; a criticism against people who spread rumors over the Internet; praise for the FDA

E. a description of SLS and SLES and their uses; known risks of SLS and SLES; criticisms aimed at SLS and SLES by detractors on the Internet; evidence that SLS and SLES are safe and the rumors unfounded.

12. The primary purpose of the third paragraph is

A. to criticize makers of personal cleansing products for including harshchemicals in their shampoos, toothpastes, and other offerings

B. to describe the way SLS and SLES work and explain why they are commonly used in various foaming products

C. to warn readers of the dangers associated with exposure to SLS and SLES, which include cancer, skin irritation, blindness, and kidney and liver ailments

D. to propose other naturally occurring substances that manufacturers could substitute for SLS and SLES in their products

E. to explain why some people fear SLS and SLES and to list the diseases that Internet rumors have linked to the substances

13. It can be inferred from the passage that the author would be most likely to agree with which one of the following statements?

A. It is unreasonable for people to be afraid of substances that have been deemed safe by the FDA and several other major organizations, and that have a long history of safe use, simply on the basis of unsubstantiated rumors.

B. Consumers can trust the FDA to make sure that all consumer products are safe because the FDA is funded by tax dollars and takes seriously its mission to ensure the health of American citizens.

C. The Internet is not a very reliable source of information on health topics unless that information has been posted by government agencies or major advocacy groups.

D. SLS and SLES are cheap and effective surfactants and emulsifiers, but they aren't especially safe to use in products intended for direct physical contact with human skin.

E. If enough concerned consumers protest the inclusion of SLS and SLES in personal care products, they can persuade manufacturers to use all-natural ingredients, but there's no reason for them to do this because SLS and SLES are safe.

Questions 14–19 refer to the following two passages. The first is adapted from Forensic Psychology and Law, by Ronald Roesch, Patricia A. Zapf, and Stephen D. Hart (Wiley). The second is adapted from Forensic Psychology: Crime, Justice, Law, Interventions, 2nd Edition, edited by Graham Davies and Anthony Beech (Wiley).

Passage A

There are many factors that may account for mistaken eyewitness identification. Wells distinguished between system variables and estimator variables. System variables affect the accuracy of (05) eyewitness testimony that the criminal justice system has some control over. For example, the way a question Is worded or the way a lineup is constructed may impact the accuracy of eyewitness identification. In these instances, the justice system has some control over these variables. Estimator variables, on the other hand, are those that may affect the accuracy of eyewitness testimony but that the criminal justice system does not have any control over. These variables have to do with the characteristics of the eyewitness or the circumstances surrounding the event witnessed. For example. the amount of attention that an eyewitness paid to a perpetrator, how long an eyewitness viewed a perpetrator, or the lighting conditions under which a perpetrator was viewed would he examples of estimator variables since they have to do with the eyewitness or the circumstances surrounding the event. The criminal justice system does not have any control over these variables. The vast majority of the research on eyewitness identifications deals with system variables since they are under the control of the justice system and thus can be modified accordingly to improve the accuracy of eyewitness identifications and testimony. Much research has shown that asking an eyewitness misleading questions will influence his or her subsequent reports of a prior observed event. Sonic theorists contend that the misleading questions serve to alter the original memory trace. Thus, a stop sign. for example, is replaced in memory with a yield sign or an empty field is replaced in memory with a field containing a red barn. Race, gender, and age are three characteristics that have been examined to determine the extent to which they impact eyewitness accuracy. Each is an estimator variable and, there-fore, out of the control of the justice system. us) With respect to age. the majority of the research has examined the differences between adults and children in terms of eyewitness testimony. Research on gender differences in eyewitness identification indicates that there is no evidence that females are any better or worse than males. Similarly, there is no evidence that members of one race arc better or worse at eyewitness identification than members of another race. However, there is evidence to suggest that people are better at recognizing the faces of members of their own race than they are at recognizing the faces of members of other races.

Passage B

Human cognitive abilities are incredible. Consider the task faced by an eyewitness who is present during a street crime. The cognitive system allows the witness to transform characteristics of the light reflected towards her eyes cos) into visual information and characteristics of perturbations in the air made by the culprit's vocal system into auditory information. The person synchronizes these sources of information (and sometimes smells, tastes, and tactile (10) information) with a highly functional knowledge base of past experiences. At later points in time, the witness is able to use this continually adapt-ing knowledge base to bring that distant information into the present. The witness may even be able to travel back to the past mentally to relive the event. What Tulving called episodic memory. As amazing as these cognitive abilities are, they are not perfect. Information is forgotten and distorted, and the past century of memory research has revealed some systematic patterns for these deficits. To understand how findings from memory research can be applied to a forensic context, it is necessary to understand how memory science works. Within a criminal context, eyewitness memory is a tool that. if reliable, should be diagnostic of guilt or innocence. By this we mean that presenting eyewitness evidence should usually make guilty people seem more likely to be guilty, and innocent people seem more likely to be innocent. To be reliable, evidence does not have to always be correct. but it should usually Be correct. In the U:S supreme court's Daubert (1993) ruling, the court argued that, for scientific evidence to be presented, there should be a known error rather, the courts do not state what the maximum error rate (or the minimum reliability) should be to allow evidence to be presented in court because this threshold would likely depend on peculiarities of an individual case.

One of the main goal for eyewitness researchers is to estimate this error rate show how it varies by different factors. Ultimately, to estimate the reliability of any forensic tool as complex and context dependent as eye witness memory, it is necessary to understand how the system works.

If a science was trying to determin the reliability of a tool to detect, for example the explosive material form a body scan device, the scientist would have the advantage that humans created the device, so the scientist could look at the blue prints. It is more difficult to understand the human cognitive system because it is the ongoing product of ad hoc engineering, a process of trial and error called evolution.

14. The author of Passage A cites research conducted to determine how all the following affect the accuracy of an eyewitness's testimony EXCEPT

A. the eyewitness's race
B. the eyewitness's gender
C. the types of questions the eyewitness is asked
D. the amount of time that has passed since the eyewitness experienced the event
E. the eyewitness's age

15. Which one of the following statements is most strongly supported by both passages?

- A. Eyewitness testimony is highly accurate considering the complexity of human memory.
- B. Eyewitness testimony is often flawed because it is influenced by a variety of factors.
- C. The human memory follows an arc pattern over one's lifetime, strengthening through adulthood and then weakening as one enters old age.
- D. Little if any evidence supports the fact that males provide more accurate eyewitness testimony than females.
- E. Determining a known error rate for eyewitness testimony involves a complex integration of many variables.

16. Which one of the following claims about eyewitness testimony is NOT suggested by Passage A?
- A. How the lighting in a particular event affects the reliability of eyewitness identification is a variable that warrants a good amount of study.
- B. The accuracy of eyewitness identification can be negatively affected by the eyewitness's race.
- C. The many factors that can lead to mistaken eyewitness identification can be grouped into two main categories.
- D. Much research has been done to assess how the order of a lineup may affect eyewitness identification.
- E. Asking misleading questions is one of the variables that affect the accuracy of eyewitness testimony over which the judicial system has at least some measure of control.

17. The passages have which of the following aims in common?
- A. to express the need for researchers to come up with a calculable error rate to determine whether eyewitness evidence may be admissible in court
- B. to define episodic memory and explain how it may come into play in judicial proceedings
- C. to identify the differences between system and estimator variables
- D. to determine how race, age, and gender can affect the accuracy of eyewitness testimony
- E. to understand how memory and human cognitive abilities are affected by a variety of different factors

18. Which of the following statements most accurately characterizes a difference between the two passages?
- A. Passage A discusses how misleading questions can affect the accuracy of eyewitness testimony, whereas Passage B dismisses the importance of how a witness is questioned.
- B. Passage A emphasizes the importance of forensic research; Passage B is primarily concerned with the way that same research influences how system variables, such as controlling lineups, are manipulated by judicial proceedings.
- C. Passage A discusses the role that race plays in greater detail than does Passage B.
- D. Both passages concern improving eyewitness accuracy, but Passage A focuses on controlling variables and Passage B concentrates on understanding the science behind human recollection.

E. Passage B focuses on how research can improve the reliability of eyewitness testimony; Passage A does not.

19. Each of the following is supported by one or both of the passages EXCEPT:
   A. Human memory sometimes fails to recollect events exactly how they happened.
   B. The cognitive system is remarkable because it is able to match sensory stimuli with previous experience.
   C. Testimony based on a witness's memory ideally should provide confirmation of a culprit's guilt.
   D. The 1993 Daubert ruling involved a court argument surrounding the need for a known error rate in regards to eyewitness testimony.
   E. Lighting issues and the length of time someone witnessed an event are examples of system variables.

Questions 20-26 refer to the following passage.

Public education as it currently known was created by a German government worried about the dangers of works uprisings that was the transformed by Enlightenment and Romantic educational theories into an institution genuinely concerned with developing human minds. Before the 1700s, Europe had no public education. Parents who wanted their children to be educated paid for private schools or private tutors. The rest of the children in Europe worked. Many of them worked alongside their parents in spinning factories, producing thread for Germany's burgeoning textile industry. The textile mill owners blatantly exploited their workers, which led to increasing levels of unrest on the part of the peasants. During the 1750s King Frederick II asked his minister of Silesia, Ernest Wilhelm von Schlabrendorff, to find a way to channel the energy of restless peasant into something that would be less dangerous to the throne.

Schlabrendorff suggested that the king could mold a compliant citizenry if he created a system of state-run schools. These schools could teach the children of the peasantry that their lot was obtained by God, that they should not try to improve it, that the government was good to the,, and that they should not questions authority, along with teaching them reading, writing and arithmetic. School would be compulsory, and children who did not attend could be punished by truant officers. This would shift children's primary loyalty from their parents and families to the state.: Their parents would be powerless against the tuant officers and thus would be forced to send their children to school whether they wanted to or not. Aristocrats liked this idea, they liked the thought of school making peasants more docile and patriotic, and they appreciated the way state-run schools would teach children of lower social classes to accept their position in life. In 1763, Frederick gave Schlabrendorff the go ahead to start opening schools and soon every child in Silesia between the ages of 7 and 15 was attending school. These earliest of school, called Spinnschulen, combined work with education. Children took classes in the mornings and spun thread in the afternoons.

By the 1800s, the Spinnschulen had metamorphosed into full day schools with state certified teachers who taught a state approved curriculum theory, much of it influence by 19th century Romanticism that directly contradicted the principle that had led to the foundation of public schools in the 1700s Johann Bernhard Basedow use the work of Enlightenment scholars to argue that education should be a holistic pursuit, incorporating physical movement, manual training, realistic teaching and the study of nature. Freidrich Froebel invented kindergarten in the mid 1800s, creating a children's garden, based on the belief that children are naturally creative and productive, and he develop special toys designed to teach specific skills and motions. Wilhelm von Humboldt specialized ins secondary and university education theory, insisting that advanced students should pursue independent research and prizing above all three educations principle: self-government by teachers, unity of teaching and academic freedom.

20. The passage is primarily concerned with discussing which one of the following?
   A. the use of public schools to disseminate political messages, as exemplified by German public schools in the 18th and 19th centuries
   B. the exploitation of the working class by German aristocracy in the 18th century and the use of public education to justify this practice
   C. the philosophical origins of public schools in 18th century Germany and the transformation in educational thinking in the 19th century
   D. the thinking of German educational theorists and their influence on modern educational practices
   E. the role of Frederick II's minister of Silesia and the German aristocracy in the creation of public schools in Germany

21. The passage suggests which one of the following about the owners of textile mills in the 1700s?
   A. They wanted their child workers to have the benefit of an education, so they opened schools within their factories and required all young workers to attend classes.
   B. Because they could pay children less than adults, they preferred to hire young workers whenever they could.
   C. They were indifferent to the well-being and needs of their workers, caring only to maximize production and profits no matter what it cost their employees.
   D. They were all aristocrats who believed their authority was divinely ordained and that, as a result of this divinely ordained position, they had a
   duty to care for the less fortunate people in their communities by providing work and education for them.
   E. They were uniformly patriotic and supported the authority of their king without question, and they advocated for the opening of Spinnschulen because this would allow peasants to be taught the same patriotic ideals they held so dear.

22. According to the passage, how did 19th-century schools differ from 18th-century schools?

A. Eighteenth-century schools were intended to make textile mills run more efficiently by making workers become more skilled at their jobs; 19th-century schools were no longer attached to textile factories.

B. Eighteenth-century schools were concerned primarily with teaching working-class children to accept their fate and love their ruler; 19th-century schools began to focus on developing the full human potential of students.

C. Eighteenth-century schools were open only to children of the aristocracy whose parents could pay their tuition. By the 19th century, schools were open to all free of charge, but poorer students had to pay their way by working in spinning factories in the afternoons.

D. Eighteenth-century schools were designed to instill patriotic ideals in the peasantry and make them docile and compliant; 19th-century schools instead tried to develop all children into free thinkers.

E. Eighteenth-century schools were not appealing to parents, who often tried to keep their children out of school and as a result were punished by truant officers; 19th-century schools, on the other hand, were appealing to both parents and children because educational philosophers believed a more pleasant environment was more conducive to education.

23. What does the author mean by the phrase "increasing levels of unrest" in Line 15?

A. riots and other forms of violence against the owners of textile factories by peasants unhappy at their treatment
B. political speeches and demonstrations by politicians trying to earn the working-class vote
C. aggression from neighboring countries looking to invade Germany
D. religious turmoil between Catholics and Protestants
E. juvenile delinquency and vandalism by unemployed and uneducated young men

24. According to the passage, what did German aristocrats think about the idea of creating public schools?

A. They feared that educating the working classes would make them less docile and accepting of their position in life and more likely to rise up and overthrow the nobles.

B. They disliked the idea of paying taxes to support public schools and resented the king and Schlabrendorff for forcing this expense on them.

C. They appreciated Schlabrendorff's brilliance in concocting an idea that would both make the peasantry more compliant and simultaneously produce more workers for the spinning factories.

D. They approved of disseminating religious education to the masses because this would make the citizenry more compliant and less likely to engage in workers' rebellions.

E. They liked the idea because it would make the peasantry more complacent and accepting of their fate, which would help keep the aristocracy safe in their prosperity.

25. According to the passage, what was the purpose of using truant officers to keep children in school?

A. to ensure that all children received the full education that was their right, even if their parents wished instead to keep them working at home
B. to take away the authority of parents and replace it with state power over children and citizens
C. to assist parents in making sure that their children attended school as required by catching and punishing children who failed to attend
D. to indoctrinate children and their parents with political messages designed to help the aristocracy
E. to assist the king and his administration in molding a compliant citizenry through a system of state-run schools

26. Which one of the following best summarizes the views of 19th-century educational thinkers?

A. The function of state-run schools is to instill obedience, patriotism, and docility in the working classes; wealthy children whose parents can afford to pay can have a more liberal education provided by private tutors.
B. The most important subject for children to learn is religion, which is why schools should be run by the Church and should include all aspects of worship and theology.
C. Most people cannot adequately educate their children on their own, but the state has an interest in an educated citizenry, so it is the government's job to provide public education and see that people send their children to school.
D. People learn best in an environment that respects their individuality, affords them freedom, and incorporates a variety of aspects of learning, such as physical movement, manual skills, and independent exploration.
E. A child's best and first teacher is his or her mother, so mothers should be encouraged to teach their children at home; this produces better results than public schools and is much cheaper for the state.

Section 4 Writing Sample

The Dawson's, a recently retired couple, would like to move from a large metropolitan area, where they have lived and worked for many years, to a smaller, slower-paced community. They are selling their three-bedroom house and plan to buy a smaller, two-bedroom condominium wherever they relocate. They are considering two possible destinations. Write an argument for either of the following two choices, keeping in mind two guidelines:

The Dawson's' income will be substantially lower than when they were working, and so they would like to reduce their living costs.

The Dawsons would like to spend their retirement enjoying a wide variety of cultural and recreational activities.

The city of Haven Hill is a popular winter resort community located about a two-hour drive from the nearest major metropolitan area. Tourists from around the world flock to Haven Hill during the winter months for downhill and cross-country skiing, and residents can enjoy hiking the trails and fishing during the quieter off-season. Haven Hill boasts a vibrant fine-arts scene and hosts a small but growing annual film festival. The average price of a condominium is about the same as the value of the home that the Dawsons are selling. During the winter season, Haven Hill condominiums can be rented to tourists on a short-term basis at a substantial premium above off-season rental rates.

The town of Brookville, about a 45-minute drive to the nearest metropolitan area, is home to Swanson College, a four-year liberal-arts institution with a prestigious music and performing arts program. The college hosts a year-round concert series featuring many well-known professional artists, and it boasts an impressive library and art gallery — both open to the general public free of charge. The city itself is a typical college town, with an extensive network of bike paths and a wide variety of low-priced eateries and retail shops catering to college students and local residents alike. Swanson College now offers a variety of inexpensive non-degree extension courses that are open for enrollment to Brookville residents. The average price of a Brookville condominium is significantly less than the home that the Dawsons are selling.

Answers 1

Section 1 Analytical Reasoning

Questions 1–5

You don't need a counter map to answer the first question in this ordering set, but you do for the remaining questions. To create an accurate counter map, first make a list of the initials of the participants' names: E, L, A, I, S, and M. (This step is especially important in this problem because the participants all have such long names.) Write out the speaking times in a row with space under them for plugging in data; go ahead and note that the 6 o'clock time slot can't contain either L or I. Then write the other rules and their contrapositives in shorthand under your counter map.

Make additional deductions based on the rules. You know that S must speak no later than 6 because she must speak before L or I. You also know that S can't speak first in the 2 slot because either L or I must speak before her

At this point, you could stop and consider the effects of a couple of possible scenarios. If L speaks at 4 and I speaks at 7, S must speak at 5 or 6. That's mildly interesting. You also know that if A speaks at 2, then S can't speak at 4, because then M would have a conflict between speaking at 7 (the last slot) and speaking before A. The rules really are quite explicit, so get going on the questions.

Just be aware that the numbering starts at 2 p.m. Many hapless students forget that the person speaking at 2 speaks first!

1. D. Ava, Martha, Liam, Sophia , Emma, Isabella

Eliminate answers that contain rule violations. The first rule specifies that Liam and Isabella don't speak at 6. Choice B . puts Isabella in the 6 spot, so it must be wrong. The second rule states that Sophia can't speak before both Liam and Isabella, so Choice E . is out. The third rule applies when Ava speaks first. Choices C . and D . put Ava in the first spot, but Choice C . fails to put Emma after Martha. The last rule applies when Sophia speaks at 4. Only Choice A . has Sophia speaking at 4, but Choice A . doesn't place Martha in the last speaking time at 7, so the only answer that doesn't violate a rule has to be Choice D ..

2. E. Martha speaks at 5.

Record the temporary condition provided by this question on your counter map. If Ava speaks at 2, Martha must speak before Emma, which means Martha can't speak last at 7. If Martha isn't in the 7 slot, Sophia can't be in the 4 slot. Sophia can't speak at 3 or 5 because then she'd have to speak before both Liam and Isabella. So Sophia must speak at 6. With Sophia in the 6 slot, you know that either Liam or Isabella must be in the 7 slot. Because Martha has to speak before Emma, Martha can't be in the 5 slot and Emma can't be in the 3 slot. You could write out the possibilities for this question like this:

Now you can see that Choices A ., B ., C ., and D . could work, so cross them out. That leaves Choice E ., which has to be false because it doesn't allow for three time slots after Martha to fit in Emma, Sophia, and either Isabella or Liam. Choice E . is correct.

3. D. At least one person speaks before Ava speaks.

When you record the temporary condition that Martha speaks at 7 to your counter map, what do you know? The contrapositive to the third rule reveals that Ava can't speak at 2 when Martha doesn't speak before Emma. Check the answers. If Ava can't occupy the 2 slot, at least one other person must speak before Ava. Choice D . says just that; one person must speak before Ava. When you consider the possible scenarios, you realize that the other answer choices are either false or merely possible:

So Choice D . is the only choice that must be true.

4. D. Sophia

You can answer this question with a quick look at your original counter map. Who can't occupy the first slot? Sophia; she can never speak at 2. The answer is Choice D ..

5. A. Emma at 3; Sophia at 6

This problem is another rule-violation question. Plug the speakers into the time slots suggested by each answer choice and see whether they work. Choices B . and C . place Ava in slot 2. You know from your work on Question 2 that when Ava speaks at 2, Sophia can't speak at 3 and Martha can't speak at 7. Cross out Choices B . and C .. Check the other answer choices with known restrictions. Choice D . places Sophia in the 4 slot. When Sophia speaks at 4, Martha has to speak at 7. Choice D . doesn't work. Consider Choice E .. If Sophia speaks at 5 and Emma at 7, no slot is available for either Liam or Isabella to speak after Sophia, because neither of them can speak at 6. What about Choice A .? You can schedule the speakers in the following order: Martha, Emma, Ava, Liam, Sophia, Isabella. Choice A . is the only possible scenario.

6. Correct answer: D. Notice that B must be with V, so the only possibility is for D to be seen on Friday with S:

7. Correct answer: A. Because A C S, if B is seen on Wednesday, then A must be seen on Monday or Tuesday.

8. Correct answer: A. B is seen with V, so D can never be seen on the same day as V.

9. Correct answer: E. None of the previous four possibilities could occur. However, E could be seen on Friday with U:

10. Correct answer: A. In this scenario, we can figure out the entire configuration of the game. The A C S relationship is pivotal in deductions:

11. Correct answer: B. S is paired with either D or E. These two variables could go on any day except immediately after S or immediately before V. U could go before or after any variable except im-mediately after S or immediately before V.

12. Do this question first in this game.

A . This puts Da and No together in group 2.

B . This is the answer; it doesn't violate any rules.

C . This doesn't put Bp with an orange.

D . This puts the two apples together.

E . Like D ., this puts the two apples together.

13. Do this on the second through the game. This is actually quite simple if you have the deduction that exactly one space in each group must be occupied by Ca, Da, or No. If you happen to peek on the first pass and see that A . is the answer, that's great. If you wait for the second or don't have the deduction, trying the choices in order will quickly lead you to discover that A . can't work.

14. Do this on the second time through the game. We can easily eliminate choices by finding counterexamples in our prior work. In fact, as it turns out, our work from question 15 alone eliminates A . B . C ., and E .. The only choice we can pick here is D ..

15. Do this on the first time through the game. Since Bp has to appear with an orange, the only way we could also have it appear with a pear is to put it into basket 3. That forces No into basket 3 also; the two apples occupy the reserved spaces in baskets 1 and 2, in either arrangement, leaving Vo for the remaining space in basket 2.

The only choice that's possible, is E ..

16. Do this on the second time through. If you happen to spot that E . would violate our crucial deduction about Ca, Da, and No, then you can pick it directly. Otherwise, we can do it using prior work. Our work from question 18 shows that A ., B ., and D . don't have to be true all the time; our work from question 15 shows that C . doesn't have to be true all the time. You can get to E . easily either way.

17. Do this on the first pass through the game. If Bp isn't in basket 3, then it can only go into basket 2; it must appear there with No. That forces the apples into the two remaining reserved spaces, in either arrangement, leaving Vo and Fp to occupy the two open spaces in

basket 3. Here's the diagram:

The only choice that's possible, given this diagram, is C ..

18. Do this on the first pass through the game. Fp and Ca in the same basket can happen either in basket 2 or in basket 3. Since this is a must-be-true question, it's probably easier to map out the two possible scenarios.

If Fp and Ca are in basket 2, then Bp must go into basket 3. The only open space is in basket 3; this space must contain Vo. Now Bp is in the same basket with an orange, so Da and No can occupy the reserved spaces in baskets 1 and 3 in either order.

If Fp and Ca are in basket 3, then Bp must go into basket 2 with No. Once again, Vo goes into basket 3; this time, Da has to go into basket one.

question:

The only choice that has to be true in both scenarios is E ., the right answer.

Questions 19–25

The first question in most logic game sets merely requires you to apply the rules to each answer. But coming up with a good, clear counter map is the key to figuring out the solutions to the remaining questions in the set. First things first — set up the game pieces using uppercase initials for the movies (E, G, I, M, and W) and lowercase letters to mark film format (v for videotape and d for disc). You may also want to add two Xs to designate the two empty days. So, you designate *Emma* on videotape as Ev and *Wuthering Heights* on disc as Wd.

Draw a table on your counter map with the nights of the week as column.

heads. Start on Friday and finish with Thursday. Note that there are seven nights and five films, so two nights are empty. Record the rules on your counter map. The easiest rule to write down is Ev in the Monday column. The second rule states that the student watches Wd before Ev, so the student can't watch Wd on Tuesday, Wednesday, or Thursday nights. Because the student watches G before both M and I, he can't watch G on Wednesday or Thursday, nor can he watch M or I on Friday.

Consider the ramifications of the final rule. If the student can't watch any two videotapes or two DVDs next to each other, he can't watch any film on Sunday. Sunday must be an empty day. You also know that he must watch W on Saturday because that's the only way he can watch it before E without violating the final rule. You can draw a further conclusion: If the student watches a movie on Friday, it must be a videotape.

See whether you can come up with more information about the other films and nights. If the student views a film on Tuesday, it must be on disc. You also know that *Great Expectations* must come before both *Ivanhoe* and *Middlemarch*, but you don't know the order of *Ivanhoe* and *Middlemarch*. You can make that work in two ways — either *Great Expectations* is the video on Friday or it's a disc on Tuesday. If *Great Expectations* is a video scheduled for Friday, then *Ivanhoe* and *Middlemarch* are discs on Tuesday and Thursday. If instead *Great Expectations* is a disc on Tuesday, then either *Ivanhoe* or *Middlemarch* is a videotape, and the other of the pair is a disc. In that case, the student would distribute *Ivanhoe* and *Middlemarch* in the proper order between Tuesday and Thursday. Note that the only possible film for Friday is *Great Expectations* on video (Gv), so if the student watches a film on Friday, that's the one. When you narrow down the possible schedules to these two, answering the questions is a piece of cake.

19. C. Friday: Great Expectations; Saturday: Wuthering Heights; Monday: Emma; Tuesday: Middlemarch; Thursday: Ivanhoe

You can usually answer the first question in the set by eliminating answer choices that violate the rules. The first condition states that the student watches *Wuthering Heights* before *Emma*. No choices violate this rule. The next condition specifies that the student watches *Middlemarch* and *Ivanhoe* after *Great Expectations*. Choice E . violates the rule by scheduling *Middlemarch* before *Great Expectations*. Eliminate Choice A . because it schedules *Emma* on Sunday. Choice D . schedules *Wuthering Heights* on Friday and no film on Saturday, which violates the rule that the student watches a film on disc for Saturday. To determine whether Choice B . or Choice C . is correct, apply the fifth condition that a video and disc can't be watched on consecutive nights to both. Choice B . schedules a disc *(Wuthering Heights)* on Saturday, which means that the film the student saw the night before *(Great Expectations)* must have been a video. *Emma* is also on video, so that takes care of the two films on videotape and means that the student views discs on two consecutive nights, Tuesday and Wednesday. That can't be. Choice C . inserts an off day between the two films that must be on disc, so it's the only answer that doesn't violate a rule.

20. A. *Great Expectations* is on disc.

The only way the student can view *Great Expectations* before *Emma* is to watch it on Friday (the first schedule listed on your counter map) because *Wuthering Heights* occupies Saturday and Sunday is off. The film on Friday must be on videotape; otherwise, it would violate the rule about putting films of the same format on days immediately before or after each other. So *Great Expectations* can't be on disc, and the answer is Choice A .. As for *Ivanhoe* and *Middlemarch,* either one of them could be on disc. You know there's no film on Sunday, and they could take place on Tuesday and Thursday, so the other four answers either must be or could be true.

Choice A . is correct.

21. C. The student watches *Great Expectations* exactly one day before watching *Middlemarch*.

If *Middlemarch* is on videotape, the student must be watching the films according to the second schedule on your counter map. So *Great Expectations* and *Ivanhoe* both must be on disc. In that case, *Great Expectations* must be on Tuesday, *Middlemarch* on Wednesday, and *Ivanhoe* on Thursday, with no film on Friday.

Of the answer choices, only Choice C . is possible. Choice A . is wrong because *Ivanhoe* is on disc. Choice B . is wrong because the student must watch *Emma* two days before watching *Middlemarch*. Choice D . is wrong because the student must watch *Ivanhoe* on Thursday. Choice E . is wrong because the student must watch *Middlemarch* on Wednesday. But he must watch *Great Expectations* exactly one day before watching *Middlemarch*, so Choice C . is correct.

22. E. The student doesn't watch a film on either Tuesday or Thursday.

Test the answers, checking them on your counter map. Eliminate those that either must be or could be true. Try Choice A .. According to the first schedule, the student could watch G on Friday and E on Monday, so that could be true. Now take a look at Choice B .. He must watch a film on Monday, and Wednesday can go either way, so it could be true that he watches films on Monday and Wednesday. Try Choice C .. He could take Friday and Sunday off, so that could be true. Consider Choice D .. He definitely skips Sunday and could take Wednesday off if he watches *Great Expectations* on Friday, so it could be true that he doesn't watch on Sunday or Wednesday. That leaves Choice E ., and it's the only false statement. Every possible schedule on the counter map requires the student to watch something on either Tuesday or Thursday. The answer is Choice E ..

23. C. The student watches *Great Expectations* before he watches *Emma*.

If the student watches *Great Expectations* after *Wuthering Heights*, he's watching films according to the second schedule on the counter map. He must watch *Great Expectations* on disc on Tuesday, and *Middlemarch* and *Ivanhoe* must fall on Wednesday and Thursday, with the Thursday film on disc and the Wednesday film on videotape. Remember, either *Ivanhoe* and *Middlemarch* can be viewed on Wednesday or Thursday. The student can't watch anything on Friday, so Choice A. must be true. Choice B. could be true if *Ivanhoe* is on videotape, which would put it on Wednesday. Choice C. must be false because *Emma* must be on Monday and *Great Expectations* must be on Tuesday; that looks like the answer. Choice D. must be true because *Great Expectations* must be on disc. Choice E. could be true because *Ivanhoe* could be on disc. Choice C. is correct.

24. A. The student watches *Great Expectations* on Friday.

With five movies and seven nights to watch them, the student can take only two nights off. One of those is Sunday; the other could be Friday or Wednesday. If he takes Wednesday off, then the first schedule on your counter map applies, and he has to watch a film on Friday. The only film he can watch on Friday is the videotape of *Great Expectations*. That means Choice A. must be true, and Choice B. is false. Choices C., D., and E. are all possible but not necessarily true.

Choice A. is the answer.

25. B. two

The schedule for Saturday, Sunday, and Monday is the same for every schedule on your counter map. The day the student sees *Ivanhoe* depends on when he sees *Great Expectations*. If he watches *Great Expectations* on Friday, then *Great Expectations* is a videotape and *Ivanhoe* and *Middlemarch* are both discs. To watch *Ivanhoe* before *Middlemarch* and avoid viewing two discs on consecutive days, the student must watch *Ivanhoe* on Tuesday and *Middlemarch* on Thursday. If, on the other hand, he watches *Great Expectations* on Tuesday, *Great Expectations* must be on disc, and his Thursday movie must also be on disc. His Wednesday film —

Section 2 Logical Reasoning

1. A fire started in a sprinter's shoes after a race. At first the author attributes the fire to friction, but upon further reflection the author decides that it was just a publicity stunt.

Correct answer: B. This is the conclusion the author comes to.

A. This point cannot be determined on the basis of the passage. The author claims only that what-ever happened was a publicity stunt.

C. This point is not stated in the passage.

D. This point is not stated in the passage.

E. This point is not stated in the passage.

2. This is a sufficient-necessary question:

1. Coconino National Tree → Hardwood

2. Hardwood Squirrel → Tail Is Fluffy or Matted

The conclusion is:

2. Coconino National Squirrel → Coconino National Tree → Hardwoods

Correct answer: D. This is true, as shown by the first sufficient-necessary statement.

A. This statement is true only of squirrels living in hardwood trees.

B. This point cannot be determined because squirrels could exit the forest to climb a softwood tree.

C. This point cannot be determined because squir-rels that do not live in the forest could enter it.

E. Nothing in the passage relates to Coconino National shrubs.

3. Cars made by French companies are more durable than cars made by U.S. companies. However, cars made by U.S. companies have an average life that is five years longer than that of French-made cars. Maybe the French are much harder on their cars than Americans are.

Correct answer: D. If this statement were true, then French cars would be destroyed more quickly even though they are more durable.

A. This statement makes a comparison between two things and nothing.

It is nonsensical and therefore is not the answer.

B. This choice is unrelated to the text and does not really explain anything.

C. This answer does not explain the discrepancy between durability and lifetime.

E. This point is irrelevant.

4. This text describes the intensity of the election process. Since candidates put so much into running for office, it is not surprising that they are very disappointed when they lose. However, all candidates should recognize the high caliber of the competition and should not feel rejected if they lose.

Correct answer: E. This answer essentially sums up the text.

A. This point is not addressed in the text.

B. This point is part of the text, but it leaves out a major part of the story: how losing candi-dates should interpret and deal with their losses.

C. Being more or less competitive is not an issue addressed in the text.

D. There is nothing said about losing candidates not being disappointed.

5. This text claims that tool commercials are extremely compelling because they appeal to the male illusion of dominance.

Correct answer:

A. This conclusion would make sense, because the text claims that tool com-mercials are incredibly successful only because they appeal to this illusion.

B. This point cannot be determined from the text. There might be fewer purchases of a par-ticular brand of tool, but it is unlikely that the frequency with which tool as a whole is pur-chased would drop if the number of advertise-ments dropped.

C. This conclusion is too extreme to be drawn from the text. Would humor be good to market caskets?

D. This point cannot be determined from the information provided.

E. This statement is probably true, but the pas-sage does not mention whether this is the case.

6. This passage states that the major reason why infants' brains are studied is to understand how their brain processes mature into adult brain processes. It would make

sense that idiosyncratic infants would not give a lot of insight into the normal maturational process of the brain, and therefore doctors might not be as interested in studying these infants.

Correct answer:

A. If this were the case, then it would be pointless for doctors interested in development to study infants with abnormal brain patterns.

B. This answer does not mean that doctors dedicated to science would ignore the other infants because they are not cute enough.

C. This point would further confuse the situation.

D. This point undermines the conclusion of the passage.

E. This does not explain why scientists would not pay a lot of attention to such infants. If anything, this should make such cases more interesting from a research standpoint.

7. John states that moving is physically and emotion-ally exhausting. He says that he has been moving, so he is physically and emotionally exhausted.

Correct answer: B. This answer restates his major thesis.

A. This point curtly states his thesis without giving enough details.

C. This is a subsidiary point of his argument.

D. This point cannot be determined on the basis of the information provided.

E. This point cannot be determined on the basis of the information provided.

8. The scientists claim that immunological disorders arise from physiological conditions, not psychological ones. Yet, it is noted that many people being treated for stress have immunological conditions. This would lead one to believe the opposite. However, it is also possible that immunological disorders lead to stress.

Correct answer: B. This statement would explain why many people with immunological disorders are also being treated for stress.

A. This answer would not explain anything.

C. This statement does not mean that the people who are going to psychiatrists were not stressed out before they went to the doctor.

D. People without immunological disorders are not relevant to a discussion of people with the disorders.

E. Just because some elements have been dis-covered that affect both things does not mean that these rare elements act consistently to link these problems.

9. This text talks about koi ponds. It claims that if you have a pond that is big enough, then all your koi will live to be at least 15 years old.

Correct answer: C. This point must be assumed, or the conclusion of the text would be invalid.

A. Nothing is said about the quality of koi as pets.

B. Koi could lose their vibrant colors patterns so long as the fish stay alive.

D. This answer choice is nonsensical.

E. Nothing is stated about what happens when koi pass the age of 15.

10. The politician claims that the purpose of law is to maximize a person's liberty so long as that liberty is not allowed to constrain the liberty of others. For this reason, there are no laws barring a per-son from harming himself or herself.

Correct answer: D. The politician says that the government may restrict a person's liberty only when that liberty results in harm to another per-son. It is the individual's, not the government's, responsibility when he or she inflicts self-harm.

A. The politician does not make this judgment.

B. The politician implies the opposite.

C. The politician specifies only harm to another person.

E. The politician begins with an instance (harming another person) that contradicts this statement.

11. The text presents a situation in which restoring a piece of art changes it and renders previous in-terpretation invalid.

Correct answer: D.

A. This choice goes too far; the text says that reevaluation is needed, not that the previous evaluations should not have been done.

B. This choice goes too far; the first part is accurate, but rendering the artist's vision invalid is not supported by the text.

C. This is not a necessary principle underlying the argument.

E. This may be true, but it is not the main principle underlying the argument.

12. The author claims that the negative implications that Valentine's Day has for single people are huge. It cannot be determined whether the author is single, but the author neglects the positive benefits that Valentine's Day might bring to couples. To justify the elimination of Valentine's Day, the author would have to show that the benefits of Valentine's Day to couples do not outweigh the harmful effects of Valentine's Day to singles.

Correct answer: D. This is the calculation upon which the argument depends.

A. The purpose of selling candy is also mentioned.

B. This determination cannot be made from the text.

C. The opposite is assumed.

E. The opposite is assumed.

13. This text claims that Logan never lost a game he pitched because of his attitude. An obvious competing reason that might explain why he never lost a game is that Logan could have been a very good pitcher.

Correct answer: B. If Logan was a terrible pitcher, then something about his attitude would be necessary to explain his success.

A. This statement does not really support the fact that Logan's attitude won games for him.

C. This choice does not necessarily mean that there were any other pitchers besides Logan who wore their hats backwards.

D. This answer would undermine the contentions of the text.

E. This information is irrelevant.

14. This text lists several commonalities among centenarians in a group. These are exercise, abstinence from drugs, and gardening. The speaker assumes that if she begins to garden, then she will also become a centenarian.

Correct answer: C. If old age caused people to garden instead of gardening increasing the likeli-hood of living to an old age, then there would be no reason for the author to begin gardening.

A. It cannot be determined that the author be-lieves gardening to be an inspirational activity; healthy, maybe, but not inspirational.

B. The passage does not assume that these are the sole factors responsible for living to a ripe old age.

D. This is not assumed by the passage.

E. This is not assumed by the passage.

15. The psychologist claims that a nature-versus-nurture debate is raging. Furthermore, the psychologist claims that people will not reach a consensus in the debate, but eventually they will stop talking about it because it is boring.

Correct answer: B. If a solution to the debate were found, then the psychologist's claims would be contradicted.

A. This answer would support the argument.

C. It does not matter what the truth is if people never find it or stop arguing about it.

D. There is still no consensus evident here.

E. This statement would support the claims made in the text.

16. This text introduces Dr. Spock, who makes the wild claim that there is no such thing as climate change from winter to summer. Based on this claim, the author claims that there is no discrepancy in the temperature between the seasons.

Correct answer: A. It is not a good or logical idea to allow the opinion of one person to change your

mind about something that you know occurs repeatedly throughout the years, especially when there is no added support for this person's claims.

B. This assumption does not occur.

C. It does not rely on the opinions of these people; it contradicts them.

D. This is not the case.

E. This is not the case.

17. This text assumes that because it is wrong to make the coach's son solely responsible for decisions affecting the team, it is wrong to allow the son any voice in decisions affecting the team.

Correct answer: E. This answer is directly analogous, because it claims that it is wrong to allow rich people to make all decisions. Therefore, it also assumes that it would be wrong to allow rich people to make any decisions.

A. This answer is completely different.

B. This answer is completely different.

C. This answer is completely different.

D. This answer is completely different.

18. Miriam agrees that dogs hear high-pitched noises better than some other mammals, but she also identifies another mammal, the bat, on which to test the theory. Observing that bats are extremely disturbed by the high-pitched whistle, she concludes that bats have an even greater response to high-pitched noises than dogs do.

Correct answer: E. She finds a group that the scientists probably did not think about and uses it to disprove their theory.

A. Miriam certainly does not use the scientific method. She merely guesses based on a one-time observation that dogs don't hear high-pitched noises as well as bats.

B. This is not true.

C. It is not clear that the bats were more dis-turbed by the noise than a dog would be. Nor is it clear that the bats could hear it better.

D. This is not true.

19. The advertising representative implies a causal connection between placing an ad in Giant Market Gains and an increase in sales. The representative further states that this will be the result for any company that places an ad in Giant Market Gains.

Correct answer: A. Comparing sales between two companies is irrelevant to the argument.

B. This weakens by showing that all companies may not get the same results.

C., D., and E. Each of these weakens by suggesting a possible alternate cause of the increase in sales.

20. Correct answer: B. This choice removes a possi-ble alternate cause for the increase in sales, thus strengthening the claim that it was caused by the ad.

A. This suggests that the ad may have been seen multiple times, but does nothing to support the conclusion that it increased sales.

C. A coupon might have drawn business, but decreased profits, so this does not necessarily strengthen the argument.

D. This suggests that Salon Harperbelieves the ad increased business, but does not show that it really did.

E. This is irrelevant.

21. The text describes two examples of behavior that will not elicit positive treatment from other people, then recommends the golden rule.

Correct answer: C. Choice C best describes this flaw. The other answer choices describe flaws that do not occur in this argument.

22. This passage discusses ways in which wireless networking has affected college campuses. It claims that the full effects have not yet been felt and that as wireless networking improves and more people "go wireless," campuses will continue to change.

Correct answer: D. Many examples are given showing how college campuses have changed be-cause of wireless networking.

A. The conclusion follows intuitively from the introduction.

B. This does not occur

C. This does not occur.

E. No competing premises are offered in the text.

23. This histamine blocker decreases allergies by 10%. A 10% decrease in allergies is noted in a nursing home, so the assumption is made that the nursing home just started using the histamine blocker.

Correct answer: B. Weightlifting increases performance by 15%, so it is assumed that a basket-ball team that has improved its performance by 15% is now lifting weights. This corresponds ex-actly to the text.

A. This is a logical statement.

C. This is different, because it states that injury is likely to decrease effectiveness by 15%. It does not say that it does.

D. This reasoning is completely different.

E. This reasoning is completely different.

24. This doctor explains that nostalgia is triggered in a part of the brain that is different from the part where other emotions are triggered. For this rea-son, the doctor claims that nostalgia must satisfy one of these three conditions: (1) It develops later in life than other emotions. (2) It is not a real emotion. (3) It is the result of something unexplained in evolutionary history. The doctor rules out the idea that nostalgia is not a real emotion, so he or she assumes that it develops later in life than other emotions and completely ignores the third possibility.

Correct answer: B. The doctor does not eliminate the possibility that the emotion is due to something unexplained in evolutionary history.

A. This is not true.

C. This is not true.

D. This is not true.

E. The evidence in support of the idea that nostalgia arose from an unexplained part of evolutionary history would not necessarily disprove the doctor's claims.

25. The stuntman claims that car crashes are more dangerous than motorcycle crashes. The dare-devil claims that motorcycle crashes are more dangerous than car crashes.

Correct answer: A. This is their point of disagreement.

B. The stuntman does not comment on this idea.

C. The stuntman does not comment on this idea.

D. This is not necessarily always going to be a point of disagreement. What about plane crashes and car crashes? Probably the stuntman and the daredevil would both agree that even though plane crashes have more metal shielding a person's body, they are more dangerous than car crashes, which have less metal shielding a person's body.

E. The stuntman and daredevil would not dis-agree with each other regarding this idea.

Section 3 Reading Comprehension

SECTION 1—READING COMPREHENSION

1. Correct answer:

A. The purpose of the passage is to discuss ECPA and why it was enacted.

B. This is an issue that is addressed in the pas-sage, but it is not the major issue of the passage.

C. The brilliance of the drafters cannot be said to have been exalted. Instead, the ECPA is said to be confusing and unusually complicated.

D. This statement is not made by the passage.

E. This point is tangentially related to the pas-sage, but not explicitly discussed.

2. Correct answer: E. Public network service providers are said to be indifferent to the rights of their users because the providers are so tenu-ously connected to the users.

A. This word is not an accurate description.

B. The service providers do not completely ignore the rights of their users; they are just disinclined to jump through legal hoops to protect those rights.

C. This word is not an accurate description.

D. This word is not an accurate description.

3. Correct answer: D. The author describes how the added importance and growth of cyberspace has created legal issues regarding privacy that are not covered by the Fourth Amendment. In order to protect the spirit of the Constitution, ECPA was drafted to outline the rights of Internet users.

A. This statement was not made in the passage. It was merely said that they are easier to gain than search warrants.

B. The passage does not say that service providers protect no rights, just that they do not protect the rights of privacy zealously.

C. This statement is not really supported by the passage; the ECPA protects rights where they de-serve to be protected, not where there is a "need for privacy."

E. This statement is not true; the statute is in-terpreted based on the intent of the drafters.

4. Correct answer: B. It was hard to tell what the Fourth Amendment would and would not allow in cyberspace.

A. The opposite was stated.

(C–E) These words do not describe the effects of the Fourth Amendment.

5. Correct answer: D. The purpose was to contrast that which the Fourth Amendment was designed to protect with that which it is currently being used to protect, namely, computers on the Internet.

A. This statement is partially true, but this is not a place where the gaps would be filled in.

B. There is no mention of cyber homes in the passage.

C. This is not the case.

E. This is not the case.

6. Correct answer: B. This is stated explicitly in lines 50–53.

A. This point is not stated or implied by the pas-sage.

C. The opposite is stated to be true.

D. This statement is not true. The Fourth Amendment still applies to our homes.

E. It cannot be determined whether this sentence is true. More than likely it is not true because the passage claimed that providers were indifferent to handing over information.

7. Correct answer: E. The passage relates the facts surrounding the dissolution of the U.S.S.R, and Russia's reemergence onto the global scene. It goes on to tell how Russia has had to change in order to adapt to the new system of government.

A. This description was true of the other governments also.

B. It was never stated that this was the only thing wrong with Russian politics.

C. It was not stated that the inability to tap into Siberian resources hurt the Soviet Union in any way.

D. This statement is true, but it is not the main idea of the passage.

8. Correct answer: D.

A. The Russian Federation came into existence after 1991.

B. According to the passage, Yeltsin came onto the scene after 1991.

C. Europe did not break up the Soviet Union. The Soviet Union was destroyed in an internal coup.

E. There was no self-governance,.

9. Correct answer: C. The "monolithic union" refers to the unified states under the Soviet Union.

A. The word monolithic is used to describe "unwieldy" and "large" instead of "stone."

B. This could be correct if the date preceded 1991, but afterward there was no sense of indestructibility.

D. This point is not mentioned in the passage.

E. This point is not mentioned in the passage.

10. Correct answer: A. This passage explains the implications of the breakup of the Soviet Union.

B. The passage makes no such claim.

C. There is no explanation of the short-term goals of the smaller republics.

D. This point was hinted at by the paragraph, but the purpose of the paragraph is to explain how the states would need to reorganize, not to cast blame.

E. There is no normative judgment made regarding the location of the capital in Moscow.

11. Correct answer: A. This view was shown by their preference to avoid living in Siberia.

B. This statement is not true. There is thought to be almost a vacuum of power in the region since the fall of the Soviet Union.

C. This inference is not accurate.

D. This is a contradiction in terms. Favorably desolate?

E. The opposite of this description is stated.

12. Correct answer: E. Nothing is said about Russia currently being benevolent or corruption free.

A. The passage makes this point

B. The passage makes this point.

C. The passage makes this point

D. This is the main point of the passage.

13. Correct answer: E. The primary purpose of the passage is to introduce and describe stem cells. Additionally, the passage emphasizes the potential importance of stem cell research to our society.

A. Diabetes is not mentioned in the passage.

B. This issue is touched upon, but its ethicality is not aggressively discussed.

C. The passage merely offers a hypothesis about the effects stem cell research may have in medicine. Additionally, the potential effects are not "hesitantly" discussed.

D. Stem cells are not considered "alternative medicine."

14. Correct answer: E. The importance of the re-search is unknown, but the potential that stem cells hold may be greater than anyone can imagine based on the small amount of research that has been conducted.

A. Putting cures into a developing fetus is not an issue that is discussed.

B. The opposite of this sentence is stated in the passage.

C. The passage never makes this claim.

D. This statement is probably true, but the passage never suggests that more donors would be needed.

15. Correct answer: A. This answer is correct because stem cells can originate in undifferentiated form and then turn into a specific type of cell.

B. Nothing about evolutionary achievement is discussed in the passage.

C. The legislature is not mentioned in the passage.

D. The passage does not offer enough informa-tion to make this assumption.

E. The passage does not suggest that stem cells can be gathered from cadavers.

16. Correct answer: D. If this statement were true, then stem cells could potentially cure any disease. This potential would certainly cause them to be-come a valuable staple of the medical community.

A. This is not convincing support that stem cells will eventually become highly beneficial in medicine.

B. This statement does not imply much of any-thing about the usefulness of stem cells.

C. This statement would undermine the con-tention that stem cells will prove to be extremely valuable to the medical community.

E. This lack of need is a good thing, but it is not relevant to how beneficial stem cells will be.

17. Correct answer: B. Scientists want to learn the basics about stem cells, which is why they want to understand their essential or fundamental properties.

A. Auxiliary means "secondary." The passage implies that scientists are looking for the basic or central qualities of the stem cells.

C. This word does not fit the meaning of the sen-tence.

D. This word does not fit the meaning of the sen-tence.

E. Unique is a good second choice, but the word different (or unique) is used next in the sentence, so it makes sense that essential refers to some-thing besides unique properties.

18. Correct answer: C. The first paragraph introduces the topic of stem cells. The second and third paragraphs discuss the features and mysteries of stem cells. Finally, the fourth paragraph discusses the future goals of the research.

A. The author does not try to call the reader to any action. The purpose of this passage is completely informative.

B. There is really only one hypothesis outlined for every claim. There is never a debate between clashing theories.

D. Nothing is attacked because of its simplicity.

E. A point of view is not discussed. A scientific frontier is analyzed.

19. Correct answer: D. The first paragraph states that the ceremony takes place in the spring.

A. Only the mother is mentioned, and in a rela-tively minor role.

B. Only Passage B lists these.

C. This is not true. The passage states that "all the children of the tribe" underwent the ceremony.

E. This statement is not supported. The passage says it is a "former" rite of the Omaha and cognate tribes. Whether other tribes perform it is un-known.

20. Correct answer: A. Both passages give requirements for undergoing the ceremony: Passage A says it is for "children of a proper age," and Passage B lists three requirements.

Choices B, C, and D apply only to Passage A. Choice E applies only to Passage B; while Passage A mentions the use of songs, it does not describe them.

21. Correct answer: E. Both passages describe a Native American ritual ceremony, each for a different purpose.

A. No argument is made to continue the practice.

B. The art employed is not the main focus of either passage.

C. There is no mention of any misconception.

D. There is no support for the idea that the rit-ual was controversial.

22. Correct answer: B. Neither passage mentions drinking any beverage.

A. The third paragraph of Passage B mentions fasting.

C. Passage A mentions facing in the four direc-tions in the third paragraph.

D. Passage A mentions the use of fire in the sec-ond paragraph.

E. Both passages mention wind; Passage A in the second and fourth paragraphs and Passage B in the third.

23. Correct answer: B. Passage B provides details about the dramatic poem mentioned at the end of the second paragraph.

A. No purpose is given, and it only describes a part of the ceremony.

C. This is not the purpose of the paragraph.

D. There is no assertion made.

E. This choice is not supported.

24. Correct answer: A. "Mediatory" refers to the role of the priest as a go-between of the celebrant and the supernatural.

25. Correct answer: C. Passage B says that the ritual celebrates a man's act that shows ability or strength of character and is recognized by his tribe. Only choice C meets these criteria.

Section 4 Writing Sample

Johnson, Stevens, & Kunam — a mid-size advertising firm seeking an experienced advertising executive to help one of its clients resonate with a younger, more tech-savvy demographic — is faced with a decision of whether to hire a bright, technologically talented up-and-comer or an older, experienced industry professional with a more traditional but less technological approach. If I were a hiring manager with Johnson, Stevens, & Kunam, I would choose Tyler, the young recent grad with experience marketing toward the firm's key demographic, over Sofia, the older, tried-and-true account executive who may be somewhat out of touch with how to connect with younger generations.

While both options bring with them their own pros and cons, the overriding consideration is that the face of advertising has changed dramatically in recent years. Old advertising standbys like television and print advertisements simply do not reach the same numbers that they once did, particularly among the younger audiences that the firm specifically mentions that the snack food client wishes to target.

What Tyler may lack in experience he makes up for in understanding of the snack company's target market. And while he may lack the years of professional experience that Sofia has, Sofia's experience is in methods that no longer reach the current audience. Tyler's experience, albeit limited, is more closely matched to the snack company's needs. His training with an innovative firm that targets college-age adults makes him a prime candidate for connecting with the technologically savvy college crowd with whom the snack food client seeks to strike a chord. Tyler's lack of time spent in the industry means that the firm could likely start him at a lower pay grade than his older, more experienced competition and that the firm could therefore invest its resources in providing him with the necessary training in any areas where he may lack knowledge.

Furthermore, despite Sofia's ad experience, she is admittedly unfamiliar with digital media and new technologies, meaning that she herself would likely require additional training and at a higher pay rate in these areas just to get up to speed. All the print and TV ad awards in the world will not be effective if the target consumers are not reading newspapers and watching

tclcvision.

Therefore, given that the advertising firm desires an employee who can reach out to a newer, younger, and more technologically savvy demographic, its best choice would be to take on the person who is more familiar with the client's target demographic. Despite

Sofia's undeniably impressive resume, teaching her new technologies and advertising techniques would be an unnecessary "reinvention of the wheel" that would likely cost the firm more money in the long run than signing on fresh new talent capable of reaching the target audience from the get-go.

Answers 2

Section 1 Analytical Reasoning

1. Do this on the first pass through the game. If 3 contains two F's, then all the rest of the cages must contain one M and one F apiece. That makes the membership of Cages 1 and 2 clear. The conditional clue doesn't provide us any information about the arrangement in Cage 4; if you don't understand this, then you definitely need to review the material on conditional clues. Here's the diagram for this

question:

Only D . is possible.

2. Do this on the second pass through the game. If you do, then you realize that you hit the jackpot in question 4. That diagram shows that A ., C ., D ., and E . are all possible, leaving us with only B .,

the right answer.

A quick inspection shows why: We deduced initially that exactly one cage can have two F's in it; choice B . would force us to make two such cages, which in turn would force two M's together in a cage.

3. Do this on the first pass through the game. You should recognize that the new information in this question triggers the contrapositive of clue 4: F in the upper berth of 4 requires us to put an F in the lower berth of 3 to keep from violating the rule. This is answer choice D .; it's also the only deduction we can make from the information in this question.

4. Do this on the first pass through the game. An M in the lower berth of 3 requires us to put an M in the upper berth of 4, because of the conditional clue. Then the remaining berths in 3 and 4 must be occupied by F's. This leaves us one M and one F to place in the open spaces in Cages 1 and 2; they can go in either arrangement.

The berths that cannot contain males are those that must contain females. The choice that lists all of these slots, and only these slots, is D ..

5. Do this on the first pass through the game. Putting F in the lower berth of Cage 2 means that all the other cages have to contain one M and one F; then the lower berth of Cage 1 contains an M. From there, we know that Cages 3 and 4 must each contain one F and one M, and we have to watch out for the conditional clue. Be careful about jumping to conclusions, though: There are three different ways the remaining elements could be arranged in Cages 3 and 4.

It's best to proceed here:

A . The lower berth of Cage 1 must contain an M.

B . The lower berth of Cage 1 must contain an M.

C . An F in the upper berth of 4 would require us to put an F in the lower berth of 3.

D . This is possible; make sure you use the conditional clue carefully.

E . Cages 3 and 4 must each contain one M and one F to follow rule 3.

Questions 6–12

First, create a counter map for this grouping set. Make a list of the game pieces: the initials of the four women — M, N, O, and P — and three men — A, B, and C. Then create a counter map that orders the dance events.

Consider the rules. You know that every event must have one member and that no member competes more than once. Every event with a pair of dancers must include one man and one woman. A dances alone, so the maximum number of pairs is two, and two women must dance solo. What else? Well, if O competes in the rumba, then A can't. Because N must be part of a pair, she must dance with B or C. You also know that the two pair events can't be back-to-back because B and C can't dance in consecutive events.

Record that what you know: There are two pairs and three solos; N is paired, which means you only need one more pair! Your main diagram may look something like this:

6. E. Mila competes in the waltz.

Record the temporary conditions imposed by this question on your game board. When Avery dances solo in the foxtrot and Jacob provides a partner for Olivia, only one event is left for Charles to compete in — the waltz. He can't do the paso doble or tango without being immediately before or immediately after Jacob. Mila must dance with Charles because she needs a male partner, and he's the only one available. So Mila must also dance the waltz. Chart what you know on the counter map:

The answer is Choice E ..

7. C. three

You're looking for the maximum number of events for Mila, so start high and work your way down. Because Henry dances alone, Mila won't have five events to choose from. Eliminate Choice E .. Olivia's already in the rumba slot, so four isn't possible. Cross out Choice D .. Could it be three? Try Henry in the foxtrot. That leaves the paso doble, tango, and waltz open. Mila could feasibly compete in any of those, as long as she dances with Jacob or Charles. Choice C . is the answer.

8. A. Henry

If solo women compete in the foxtrot and paso doble, they must be Madeleine and Avery because Olivia is booked for the rumba and Mila dances as part of a pair. The only dance left for Henry is the tango because Olivia and either Charles or Jacob are competing in the rumba. The only spot left for the other member of the Charles-Jacob duo is the waltz with Mila. Your counter map for this question looks like this:

The answer must be Choice A ..

9. B. Charles, Jacob, and Mila

You know that both Jacob and Charles must dance with partners because you need two pairs with one man in each and Henry dances solo. The only answer that contains both Charles and Jacob is Choice B ..

10. E. Madeleine, Olivia, and Avery

When you know that two women must dance solo, you know the answer can't be Choice A . or Choice B .. Unfortunately, none of the other answers include Mila, who would be a dead giveaway that the answer was wrong. You already know from Question 9 that both Madeleine and Avery can compete solo, so Choice C . has to be wrong. To choose between

Choices D . and E ., ask yourself whether Olivia can compete solo. Sure — if, for example, Avery and Charles dance the paso doble and Mila and Jacob compete in the waltz, Olivia is on her own for the rumba. So the correct answer is Choice E ..

11. B. foxtrot and tango

Add the temporary conditions to your counter map. When Mila dances the waltz and the females dance consecutively, the females must dance the paso doble, rumba, tango, and waltz. That puts Henry alone in the foxtrot. You can eliminate any answer choice that doesn't include the foxtrot:

Choices C . and E .. Jacob or Charles must compete in the waltz with Mila because Mila needs a partner. The remaining Jacob or Charles can't dance the tango right before the waltz, so he must dance either the rumba with Olivia or the paso doble with Madeleine or Avery. That means a solo woman must perform the tango. Either the paso doble or the rumba will be the third solo, but you don't know which. Your counter map reveals the two possible arrangements of the solo events:

So the foxtrot and the tango are the only events that must have solo performers, and the answer is Choice B ..

12. E. Mila competes in the foxtrot.

Add the temporary rule that the three men dance the first three dances to your counter map. Neither Jacob nor Charles can dance the paso doble because they can't dance consecutively. So Henry dances the paso doble. You also know that Mila must dance the foxtrot with either Jacob or Charles. Your diagram for this question looks like this:

Mila must dance the foxtrot, so the answer is Choice E ..

13. Correct answer: D. G, D, E, and A is a possible group.

A . If A is on team 1, then F must be on team 2.

B . If B is on team 2, then D must be on team 1.

C . E cannot be on team 2 with F.

E . If A is on team 1, then B is on team 2.

14. Correct answer: C:

15. Correct answer: A.

16. Correct answer: E.

17. Correct answer: E. This question is very easy because the last constraint states that E can never be with F.

18. Correct answer: C. Three players who could go on team 2: C, G, and H.

19. Correct answer: A. For D and A not to be required to be on the same team, then A has to be on team

Questions 20-25

20.

A. This follows all the rules; note that it satisfies the JF block by making J perform fifth and F perform sixth. This is the answer we want.

B. This puts F in 4/9.

C. This doesn't have J perform immediately before F.

D. This doesn't have J perform immediately before F; it also doesn't have J perform after I.

E. This has G perform immediately before H.

21. Do this on your second pass through the game. Although it is a specific question, the task here looks like a difficult one, since you must directly deduce the answer. It turns out not to be as difficult as it looks. F in 3/8 means J must be in 2/7, so that we preserve the JF block. This forces I to be in 1/6 to stay in front of J. To prevent G from coming immediately before H, we must put G in 5/10 and H in 4/9, the only two spaces remaining.

We've deduced the position of every element, so A. is the answer here.

21. Do this on your first pass through the game. J in 4/9 means F must be in 5/10 to preserve the JF block. Many arrangements of I, G, and H will work from here, but we must always be certain to keep G from coming immediately before H. Although we have only one real deduction, the only choice this deduction doesn't eliminate is D..

22. Do this on your second pass through the game. As it turns out, our work on question 20 leads us directly to B., the answer here.

If instead you worked this one out, the initial deductions from the game would eliminate A., D., and E.. You can see the reason C. doesn't work if you play with it a bit: H in 5/10 means that G can't be in 4/9; we have a clue that tells us F can't appear in 4/9; in order to make the JF block, we couldn't put J in 4/9. The only element left for this space is I, but this would force I to appear after J, violating a rule.

However you arrive there, B. is the choice to pick.

23. Do this on your second pass through the game. One of our initial deductions was that F can't be in 2/7, so B. is the answer here.

24. Do this on your first pass through the game. It's unusual to find more than one Grab-a-Rule question on a game, but that's what this is.

A. This doesn't have J perform immediately before F.

B. This has G perform immediately before H.

C. This follows all the rules; it's the answer we want.

D. This puts F in 4/9.

E. This has J performing before I.

Section 2 Logical Reasoning

Section I: Logical Reasoning

1.B. This catalog is economical only when its normal prices are marked down more than occasionally.

The review must be assuming that it's impossible that the prices in this catalog can save customers money without being specially marked down. Choice A . is wrong because the argument doesn't depend on the behavior of the catalog's competitors. Choice B . looks correct. The review must assume this catalog's prices are cheap only when marked down. Choice C . isn't right. When the catalog does mark down its prices, customers evidently save money. Choice D . is wrong because this argument isn't about the catalog's competitors. Choice E . doesn't work because the argument doesn't address mail-order purchasing as a whole, nor does it propose what the customers should do. Choice B . is correct.

2. E. None of the pieces of evidence point directly to the conclusion, and all of them could lead to different conclusions.

The conclusion is that the settlement was destroyed in war. The evidence, though, doesn't seem that clear. It's not a circular argument, because the author doesn't state upfront that he thinks the settlement perished in war, so Choice A . is wrong. Choice B . doesn't work. Yes, the evidence is varied and the conclusion is unified, but that's what conclusions are supposed to do:

bring together varied evidence into a single conclusion. Choice C . is wrong because the argument doesn't contain any intermediate conclusions. Choice D . is wrong because the argument doesn't make any historical conclusions. Choice E . is the best answer; it's by no means certain that these bits of evidence point to one single conclusion.

3.C. The degree of erosion to which a coastline is subject is related to the shape of the sea bottom.

Choice A . doesn't look right. If fetch is the length of the surface of the water, it shouldn't be related to the shape of the sea bottom. Choice B . definitely seems wrong because the statements only state the factors (wind velocity and fetch) that influence wave size; there's nothing to suggest that wave size stays close to an average. Choice C . does make sense because the impact of waves is related to the shape of the sea bottom, and the coast's erosion is related to the impact of waves. Choice D . is wrong because the size of waves comes from wind and fetch, not the shape of the bottom. Choice E. looks wrong, too. Wind velocity creates size of waves, size of waves affects impact, and impact affects erosion, so average velocity of wind playing no role in erosion doesn't make sense. Choice C. is the best answer.

4.D. It is used to explain a consideration that may be taken to undermine the argument's conclusion.

The historian is arguing that for historians, seeing one event as an inevitable consequence of another is a mistake. The phrase in question explains that the historians' position of looking back on events results in their erroneous belief that, because one event precedes another, a prior event necessarily causes the later event. Choice A. is wrong; a "theoretical imperative" sounds like a requirement, and this statement is an explanation. Choice B. isn't an illustration of the premise, which would be an example of a historian making this kind of mistaken attribution of causation. The statement doesn't support any claim, so Choice C. is wrong. Choice D. seems to make sense. The historian is explaining that, although historians sometimes see events as inevitable consequences of other events, that's just an occupational hazard of the historical profession and not justified. Choice

E. is wrong. The conclusion is that historians can't in fact assert that events follow one another inevitably. Choice D. is the best answer.

5. D. When agricultural production is market-driven, it is likely to respond to rising demand by increasing production.

The speaker concludes that Chinese production will rise if demand requires it based on the premise that Chinese production is now market-driven. Clearly the author connects market-driven methods with matching supply and demand. Choice A. isn't right because it isn't actually about the difference between global and regional markets but about China's transformation to a market economy. Choice B. doesn't justify the conclusion but explains how things worked under China's older system. Choice C. is wrong because the speaker isn't talking about local production. Choice D. looks like the right answer. The speaker bases his conclusion on the principle that a market economy will respond to increased demand with increased production. Choice E. isn't right. The speaker doesn't mention inefficiency or even compare a market-driven system to a centrally regulated one; he's only interested in the effects of

China's transition between the two. Choice D . is the best answer.

6.A. It is a specific example of a general condition described in the course of the argument.

The economist argues that, because patients need medical care and hospitals, regardless of what those services cost, hospitals and doctors rather than insurers bear the brunt of cost-containment measures; the MRI statement provides an example. Choice A . is a good answer; the statement is a specific example of capital demands (MRIs and buildings) of the general condition of fiscal discipline described in the argument. Choice B . doesn't work because the MRI statement doesn't counter an attack. Choice

C . isn't as good an answer as Choice A .. The author's claim or conclusion is that health insurers are still profiting from healthcare while doctors, hospitals, and patients are being increasingly squeezed, but the MRI statement doesn't indirectly support that claim. Choice D . doesn't work. Patients' needing treatment isn't a social side effect but a normal event that remains consistent, regardless of changing circumstances. Choice E . is wrong; the MRI statement doesn't introduce the conclusion about the immunity of health insurers. Choice A . is correct.

7.B. that no other explanations exist for the decreasing revenues from CD sales

To make her conclusion, the author must assume that PTP file-sharing was entirely or largely responsible for the drop in sales of CDs. She doesn't mention copyright issues, so Choice A . is wrong. Choice B . looks like the right answer. Choice C . isn't at issue; the argument doesn't address the rights of musicians or producers to profit. Choice D . is a possibility, but it's not as good as Choice B .. It's not obvious that the author specifically assumes that people who download music would purchase it on CD if they couldn't download it. People may have downloaded far more pieces of music than they would have purchased on CDs. Choice E . doesn't really fit with the argument, which isn't about complex relationships in the music market but about how file-sharing has killed the record industry. Choice B . is best.

8.B. fails to take into account any practical factors that may limit the number of redundant systems or practical trade-offs involved in increasing levels of redundancy

The engineer believes that the more redundant control systems an airplane has, the safer it will be. But what if having so many control systems can cause problems of its own or costs more than it's worth, either in economic or practical terms? Choice A . is wrong; the engineer does think that simultaneous failure can occur, which is why he believes multiple systems are necessary. Choice B. looks like it could be the answer because it addresses problems involved with redundancy itself. Choice C. is wrong. The engineer is discussing control surfaces, so he's not obligated to consider other safety considerations. Choice D. is wrong. The engineer discusses airplane safety and isn't obligated to apply these concepts to other projects. Choice E. is also wrong because the argument doesn't depend on being able to evaluate relative levels of safety. Choice B. is correct.

9. E. Allowing employees to take leave for family matters reduces absenteeism, improves morale, and surprisingly increases productivity because the employees who are granted leave tend to work much harder and more efficiently when they come back to work.

To weaken the argument, look for an answer showing that allowing family leave doesn't hurt productivity or perhaps even helps it. Choice A. doesn't affect the argument because standard of living isn't an issue, and it doesn't mention workplace productivity. Choice B. could arguably weaken the argument because it provides evidence that workers may not abuse the privilege of leave — fathers aren't taking family leave at all, which weakens the conclusion that workers would work less if they had leave. On the other hand, if taking paternity leave angers coworkers, that strengthens the conclusion that family leave hurts workplace morale, so this isn't the best answer. Choice C. strengthens the argument by showing that FMLA leave costs the employer money. Choice D. also strengthens the argument by illustrating the destruction caused by one employee leaving for a while. Choice E. weakens the argument. If employers are worried about productivity and morale, this choice says that allowing leave actually increases productivity and morale. Choice E. is the right answer.

10. A. Businesses profit from casino gambling because they take in money from local and visiting gamblers, whereas local individuals have more opportunities to lose money gambling.

Look for an answer that may explain why counties with casinos have thriving businesses but bankrupt individuals. Choice A. looks right.

Businesses take in money from gamblers (who aren't all local), and locals give their money to casinos. Choice B. doesn't help. Casino odds may explain why gamblers would go bankrupt but not why businesses would profit. Choice C. explains why businesses thrive but not why individuals suffer. Choice D. explains gamblers' losses but not businesses' gains. Choice E. may help explain why individual bankruptcy rates are so high in areas with casinos but does nothing to explain the profitability of businesses in those areas. Choice A. is the best explanation.

11. E. Some food stamp recipients say they prefer the paper coupons because they can't tell how much money they have in their debit card accounts.

Eliminate answers that support the position that debit cards are better than paper coupons. Choice A . supports the argument by showing how the new debit cards increase participation. Choice B . supports it by showing how paper coupons were often used for fraud. Choice C . supports the worker's position because the debit cards can be used only for approved items. Choice D . supports it because it shows how the cards are much more convenient, which will increase participation. Choice E . is the only answer that doesn't support the social worker's position; it presents a disadvantage of the debit cards. Choice E . is correct.

12. C. It highlights the importance of this discovery because it disproves a long-held theory about hibernation.

This discovery of an animal that hibernates in hot weather may be groundbreaking, especially if previous scientific wisdom held that hibernation only happens in cold weather. Choice A . is wrong because the belief being challenged isn't that primates never hibernate but that animals never hibernate in the heat. Choice B . isn't right because the assertion isn't an accusation of any kind. Choice C . makes the most sense because it's an important discovery. Choice D . is wrong. The primatologist never disputes the conclusion that the behavior is in fact hibernation. Choice E . doesn't work because the primatologist isn't setting up a rival theory in a deliberate ploy to attack it. Choice C . is right.

13. C. To increase sales, having a famous actor in the title role of a film is more important than having an actor who can speak the film's language.

Wow, that's a gamble, casting an English-speaking actor in an Italian movie

and letting him speak his part in English while everyone else speaks Italian. But the director must have his reasons; he clearly thinks that Lancaster's fame is a more valuable commodity for sales than an ability to speak Italian would be. He must not think that Italian audiences would refuse to see the film with Lancaster or he would never cast him, so Choice A . is wrong. Choice B . may be true, but actors' objections don't seem to be the director's concern. Choice C . is right — the director obviously believes fame is more important to box-office success than Italian ability. Choice

D . is beside the point. The director doesn't think coaching Lancaster in Italian is necessary. Choice E . is also beside the point; maybe Lancaster would feel uncomfortable, but the director isn't concerned about that here. Choice C . is correct.

14. E. The only substances that could eradicate all mosquitoes would also kill off many birds and beneficial insects.

George suggests that, because losing a single species won't hurt an ecosystem, eradicating mosquitoes will cause no environmental problems. Look for an answer that disproves this. Choice A . is a reason in favor of eradicating mosquitoes. Choice B . doesn't strengthen or weaken the argument because it concentrates on the effect of restoring wetlands on the mosquito population rather than the effect that eradicating the mosquito population would have on wetlands. Choice C . provides another strike against mosquitoes and may strengthen the argument. Choice D . may suggest that mosquitoes do play a role in the ecosystem, but by itself it doesn't really hurt George's argument. The answer could weaken the argument if it were more specific, such as providing evidence that mosquitoes are the only thing some birds eat. Choice E . does weaken George's conclusion. If the only way to eradicate mosquitoes would inevitably devastate birds and other insects, then George can't suggest that his proposal would have no environmental costs. Choice E . is right.

15. E. large numbers of people coming to a park prevent individuals from enjoying use of the park

The author assumes that large groups in parks are bad, but she gives no reasons for this claim; she just assumes that they're bad and shouldn't be in the park. She implies but doesn't directly state that large groups somehow interfere with all citizens' equal rights to the park. Choice A . is wrong because the author doesn't suggest that large groups are noisy or violent.

She mentions no complaints, so Choice B . is wrong. Choice C . goes against her argument, so it's wrong. Choice D . likewise weakens her argument, so it's wrong. Choice E . is the only answer that makes sense. If she's assuming that large groups interfere with individual citizens' enjoyment of the park, then the groups would be a problem. Choice E . is correct.

16. D. Funds saved in FSAs must be spent during the plan year or forfeited.

Choice A . looks like a reason why employees should use FSAs. Choice

B . offers an explanation of why there may not be widespread employer participation in FSAs, but it doesn't explain why many of those employees who have the opportunity to participate in FSAs choose not to. Cross out Choice C . because it's another clear benefit of FSAs. Choice D . is a drawback of FSAs and may well explain why few employees use them.

Choice E. describes a trend toward FSA participation and therefore doesn't explain why so few employees currently use FSAs. Choice D. is the best answer.

17. C. A majority of residents of these six Latin American countries do not believe that democracy is necessarily the best form of government for them.

It appears from this argument that many Latin American people don't like their democratic governments. Choice A. provides additional support for the argument but doesn't draw a conclusion from the statements provided.

Choice B. offers an explanation for the residents' dissatisfaction with their governments but doesn't sum up the argument. Choice C. makes sense as a conclusion; if the people are willing to substitute democratically elected leaders with a dictator, they must not be impressed with their leadership. Choice D. introduces a side issue and is too specific to be a conclusion. Choice E. supplies evidence that would support the conclusion but isn't itself a conclusion. Choice C. is the best answer.

18. B. The relationship between salmonella and eggs has in fact changed over the years, justifying the recent caution with which people regard raw eggs.

The argument is about the changed risk of salmonella. In the past salmonella was only on the outside of eggs, but now it's inside the eggs themselves. Choice A. can't conclude the argument because the author

doesn't specifically state that salmonella has increased, only that its means of transmission has changed. Choice B. makes sense as the conclusion; it sums up the argument's premise that changes in the way salmonella presents itself in eggs has altered the way people must handle eggs as food. Choice C. isn't right. The author isn't suggesting that salmonella can't be serious, only that it's rarely fatal. Choice D. doesn't quite work, because the author doesn't describe any change in egg production, only a change in the chickens producing them. Additionally, it doesn't address the egg preparation changes people have had to make. Choice E. isn't right either. People in the past ate raw eggs safely because the eggs were uncontaminated, not because people were blissfully ignorant that the eggs contained salmonella. Choice B. is best.

19. A. Operating systems with generous amounts of memory are less susceptible to crashing, even when applications are poorly written.

Okay, you want to find the four answers indicating that operating systems are responsible for the smooth functioning of applications and are able to somehow manage their memory problems. The best way to do this is by process of elimination. If you can find four answers that show the operating system handling applications' memory issues, then the answer that's left over should be correct. Choice B. helps the conclusion because it shows that operating systems are responsible for handling the memory used by individual applications. Choice C. helps because it shows that operating systems can spot overuse of memory and stop it. Choice D. helps because it tells you that programmers should know how to program an operating system that can prevent memory errors, which means all operating systems should be able to do this. Choice E. helps the conclusion because it describes what an efficient operating system should be able to do. Choice

A. is the only answer that doesn't put responsibility for memory management on the operating system; adding memory to the computer evidently can let the operating system off the hook. Choice A. is the right answer.

20. D. Ted's parents have stated that he cannot drive the station wagon unless it is to Alice's house. When his mother saw the station wagon parked at the mall, some miles away, Ted argued that Alice was not at home. Ted's mom pointed out that he ought, upon discovering that fact, to have driven straight home.

This question is a tough one, requiring lots of reading and thinking. Company A has a limited license to use a product but violates the license, claiming it's invalid. But there's another rule beyond the license that makes Company A's actions wrong, even if the license is invalid. So General Rule (GR) states an action can't be taken; Limited Rule (LR) provides an exception to GR in certain circumstances. Party A violates LR by taking action and says it's okay because LR is invalid. Party A is still wrong because action violates GR. Look for an answer that follows this pattern. Choice A.'s scenario provides GR (warranty). Party A (consumers) took an action that appeared to be endorsed by another document. Party A successfully proved it didn't violate GR. Because Party A prevails, the pattern can't be the same. Choice B. provides GR (no 13-year-olds are allowed into NC-17 movies). The ticket seller made a mistake, which isn't the same as authorizing an LR exception, so the pattern breaks down in this scenario. Choice C. portrays the attempt of Party A (the manager) to create a LR for the GR of the distilled liquor license. The authority states that the LR doesn't exist. This situation isn't the same as the original. Evaluate Choice D.

The GR is that Party A (Ted) can't drive the station wagon. The LR is that he may drive it to Alice's house. Party A violates LR but says it's okay because LR wasn't available. The authority (Mom) says Party A is still wrong because he violated GR. Even though Ted's situation is very different in subject matter from the original, it follows the same rule pattern. Choice D. is likely the best answer. Choice E. doesn't establish an LR for Party A to violate. The celebrity didn't grant permission to the magazine to photograph him in any circumstances, so the pattern is different. Choice D. is correct.

21. B. No single written edition of a Greek epic can claim to represent the "original" version.

The author's conclusion is that texts of poems differed from place to place because of the changes in oral transmission of the same stories. Choice A. is clearly wrong because the scholar isn't suggesting that each classical epic had one original text. Choice B. looks right because the scholar argues that there can't be any "original" text but instead many written versions of the same epics. Choice C. doesn't make sense. The scholar doesn't mention narratological complexity. Choice D. doesn't work, either, because the scholar doesn't imply that people stopped transmitting epics orally after the poems were written down but in fact suggests the opposite — that they continued to compose even after they began transcribing. Choice E. is totally wrong; the scholar gives no suggestion of political influence in the argument. Choice B. is correct.

22. E. If people see online images of items in the museum's collection, they will no longer be interested in seeing the collection with their own eyes.

The curator seems to assume that if people see the images online, they won't have any interest in visiting in person. Choice A. isn't the point because the curator isn't worried about damaging the images. Choice B. doesn't work because the curator doesn't mention a concern for decreased revenue. Choice C. likely isn't the curator's concern. He isn't specifically worried about the extent of online distribution but rather its effect. Check the remaining answers to see whether you have a better option. Choice D. isn't his concern, either, because he doesn't mention quality issues. Choice

E. is the best answer. The curator is worried that online publication of the images will remove the incentive to visit the actual museum in person. Choice E. is best.

23. A. Spousal and marital difficulties were formerly responsible for a large number of premature returns from foreign assignments.

If helping spouses has improved expatriate retention by such a huge amount, then unhappy spouses must have previously been responsible for lots of premature returns. Choice A. looks like a good answer. If unhappy spouses contributed to employees' leaving international assignments, helping spouses adjust would improve the situation. Choice B. is wrong. If spouses are already thrilled with the international experience, their dissatisfaction is unlikely to contribute to employees' leaving their overseas posts. Choice C. would support the argument, but it's too specific to be a necessary assumption on which the conclusion depends (there could well be other reasons why spouses are dissatisfied). Choice D. doesn't explain why helping spouses has improved retention. Choice E. provides an example of what companies are doing to help spouses but isn't the assumption that links the argument's premises to the conclusion. Choice A. is the best answer.

24. E. You catch more flies with honey than you do with vinegar.

Now, this is a nice little question — a story and some proverbs. You have to decide which proverb — principle — matches the traveler's experience. A stitch in time saves nine means that early correction of problems prevents

them from getting bigger; that doesn't really fit here, so Choice A. is wrong. Don't price an unborn calf means you shouldn't depend on an event that hasn't yet occurred; that's not right, so Choice B. is wrong. Choice C. may work because the traveler does carry his computer with him, but it doesn't explain the comparative reaction of the clerk. Choice D. is wrong because the traveler isn't borrowing or lending anything. Choice E. is the best answer; because he was nice (honey) to the clerk (the fly), she was nice to him and punished the rude (vinegar) travelers by dawdling.

Section 3 Reading Comprehension

1.D. Manning's work exemplifies how biography can be a powerful tool for a historian of science, who can use the genre to explore the effects of politics, economics, and emotions on the direction of scientific development.

This passage is mainly about the effectiveness of biography as a genre for exploring the history of science and the importance of analyzing scientific discoveries from a historical perspective. The business about Black Apollo is just an example the author uses to illustrate his point. So Choice A . is wrong because the passage's main point isn't the importance of Ernest Everett Just. Choice B . is a point the author makes in the last paragraph, but it's not the entire passage's main point. Choice C . appears in the second paragraph, but once again, it doesn't cover the whole passage. Choice D . looks like the right answer; it sums up the overarching theme of the passage. Choice E . is wrong because, like Choice A ., it focuses too much on Black Apollo. Choice D . is correct.

2.A. illuminate the effects of social forces on scientists in a way that scientists themselves are unlikely to do

According to the author, "One of the central principles of the history of science, indeed a central reason for the discipline, is to show that science is a product of social forces." That makes Choice A . look like a very good answer. Choice B . isn't exactly right. The author says people can learn scientific theories by reading the work of the scientists themselves. The drawback is that the picture given by scientists is incomplete because it ignores historical context. Choice C . is also imprecise. Historians of science do write biographies, but biographies are just one way to accomplish their main goal of revealing the social forces behind scientific discovery. Choice D . is wrong because the author never suggests that historians of science want to influence scientific research. Choice E . is likewise wrong. History of science exists to analyze science as a part of society, not to make science palatable to non-scientists. Choice A . is right.

3.C. to explain why biography is both a popular historical genre and a powerful medium for explaining the significance of scientific discoveries

The second paragraph contains a discussion of biography as a historical genre and lists its many advantages. Choice A . isn't at all the main point. It just barely appears in the paragraph. Choice B . is wrong; the author does believe biography is a good historical form for the historian of science. Choice C . looks like a good answer. Choice D . is incorrect; the author says that biographies are very good for teaching children. Choice E. never appears anywhere. Choice C. is right.

4.A. One of the best ways to come to an understanding of the realities of race relations and scientific development in the 20th century is to read an in-depth account of the life of one of the people who lived and worked in that world.

Choice A. looks pretty good; this is in fact what the author has been saying about the history of science. Choice B. is wrong. The author doesn't think historians should glorify their subjects and notes that Manning doesn't glorify Just. Choice C. is also wrong. The author doesn't imply that a scientific history should downplay science simply because it's "history." Choice D. isn't right. The author explicitly says that Just wasn't the most significant scientist of his time. Choice E. contradicts what the author says in the second paragraph. Choice A. is the best answer.

5.D. Just's daily experiences illuminate the conditions characterized by both scientific research and racial relations during his lifetime.

Here's what the passage says: "A comprehensive appreciation of the conditions that Just faced in his daily work offers a powerful lens through which to examine the development of science and racial boundaries in America." Choice D. looks like the answer that matches best with this statement. The other answers are all true, but they're also incidental, facts that add up to a bigger picture but by themselves aren't enough to create a significant history.

6.E. the straightforward organization of a biography, which follows the course of the subject's life

A biography is a story of a person's life; the format can't change that much. The author says, "Biographies simply tell a story." The phrase "simplicity of form" doesn't refer to language, so Choice A. is wrong, nor does it mean page design, so Choice B. is wrong. It doesn't mean simple writing style, so Choice C. is wrong. Choice D. is wrong because the author suggests that a biography's power exists despite its simplicity. All the author means is that biographies have a standard format, which is fairly consistent from book to book; that makes Choice E. correct.

7.C. SLS and SLES are detergents that are commonly used in personal care products because they are effective and safe, despite unsubstantiated rumors to the contrary.

This passage introduces the reader to a couple of detergents commonly used in numerous household products. It describes how they work and mentions a few hazards associated with them. The reason the author mentions those hazards in the second paragraph is to get the facts in ahead of the risks that are solely based on rumor, because her point in the last paragraph is that many of the things people fear about SLS and SLES aren't based on fact. She obviously thinks SLS and SLES are safe as they're commonly used and believes that approval by the FDA and other scientific organizations is sufficient proof of this safety.

Choice A . is a possible answer, but it ignores the discussion of Internet detractors, so it doesn't cover the entire passage. Look for something with a more global application. Choice B . is wrong. The presence of "despite" suggests that the author thinks incorporating SLS or SLES into personal care products is irresponsible or dangerous, which isn't justified by the passage. Choice C . looks like a better answer than Choice A . because it incorporates more of the passage's information. Choice D . is wrong because this passage isn't about the Internet rumors but about counteracting them. Choice E . is wrong. It's true that the author doesn't have a problem with using SLS in both shampoo and engine degreasers, but that's not the main point of the passage. Choice C . is the best answer.

8. B. shampoo, toothpaste, bathroom cleaners, and engine degreasers

You have to read carefully to answer this one. Don't assume any product contains the substances unless the passage tells you so. If you prefer, you can underline or circle substances that the author mentions in the passage in the answer choices — that makes it easier to see the ones that appear in the text. Choice A . is wrong because the author never mentions mouthwash, sunscreen, or hair dye. Choice B . looks good. They're all mentioned in the passage. Choice C . is wrong because the passage doesn't mention engine lubricants. Choice D . is wrong because moisturizer and baby wipes don't appear. Choice E . is wrong because fabric softener isn't in the passage,

though you could probably infer that SLS and SLES are found in kitchen cleaners and laundry detergents. Choice B . is correct.

9. E. refute claims that SLS and SLES are dangerous

The author says that the rumors about SLS and SLES are absurd and unsubstantiated and "the FDA has approved the use of SLS and SLES in a number of personal care products."

That means she's using FDA approval as evidence of the substances' safety. Choice A. looks like a possible answer, though it doesn't mention the author's suggestion that the FDA approval implies safety, so it misses the reason why the author brings up the FDA. Choice B. is wrong because even though the author thinks that the FDA has the best interests of consumers in mind, that isn't the reason why the author mentions the FDA. The purpose of mentioning the FDA is to provide evidence debunking the Internet myths. Choice C. doesn't work because the author isn't in fact suggesting that FDA approval of putting SLS and SLES in personal care products means that manufacturers don't have to test these products for safety. Choice D. is wrong; the author isn't criticizing the FDA in any way — quite the contrary. Choice E. works the best because the author mentions the FDA to achieve the larger goal of debunking the Internet rumors. Choice E. is correct.

10. D. burning eyes, burned skin after long exposure, and diarrhea if ingested in large quantities

Read the passage carefully. The answers to this question appear in the second paragraph, not in the third paragraph, which lists risks that haven't been proven. Skim the answer choices to cross off anything that appears in the third paragraph. Choice D. is the right answer. Every other choice contains ailments that Internet rumors have associated with SLS and SLES but that haven't been substantiated.

11. E. a description of SLS and SLES and their uses; known risks of SLS and SLES; criticisms aimed at SLS and SLES by detractors on the Internet; evidence that SLS and SLES are safe and the rumors unfounded

Look for an answer that could function as an accurate ordering of all paragraphs in the passage. Choice A. isn't quite right because it leaves off the subject of the first paragraph. Choice B. is wrong. The passage doesn't contain any anecdotal accounts of SLS injuries. Choice C. doesn't work because the first paragraph doesn't describe the chemical composition of

SLS and SLES. Choice D. isn't quite right because it doesn't mention the known and unsubstantiated risks associated with the substances. Choice E. is the best answer because it follows the structure of the passage closely.

12. E. to explain why some people fear SLS and SLES and to list the diseases that Internet rumors have linked to the substances

The third paragraph discusses the Internet rumors that hold SLS and SLES responsible for a host of ailments without providing proof. The author obviously wants to discredit these rumors; that's what the last sentence is all about. She's not criticizing, so Choice A. is out. She's not describing the substances — that's in the first paragraph — so Choice B. is out. She doesn't believe these risks are real, so she's not warning anyone of anything, and Choice C. is out. She makes no proposals of alternate substances, so Choice D. is out. Choice E. is the best answer here.

13. A. It is unreasonable for people to be afraid of substances that have been deemed safe by the FDA and several other major organizations, and that have a long history of safe use, simply on the basis of unsubstantiated rumors.

Choice A. looks like a good possibility. The author does seem to think it's silly to believe rumors about substances that people have been using safely for years. Choice B. doesn't quite work. The author does trust the FDA but makes no mention of its sources of funding or mission. Choice C. is wrong. While the author clearly thinks that some Internet information isn't trustworthy, the passage doesn't provide sufficient information for you to infer how she feels about information available about other health topics. For example, she could easily think that the Internet supplies good information on heart disease. Choice D. doesn't work. The author does think SLS and SLES are cheap and effective surfactants and emulsifiers, but she doesn't think that they're unsafe to use in products that contact human skin. Choice E. is wrong. The author probably wouldn't want to prevent manufacturers from using SLS and SLES in their personal care products, but there's no reason to believe that she thinks enough protests could stop this inclusion. She doesn't mention protests anywhere in the passage. Choice A. is the best answer.

14. D. the amount of time that has passed since the eyewitness experienced the event

Answer this question by eliminating answers that Passage A indicates have been researched to discover their effect on the accuracy of eyewitness testimony. The third paragraph comes right out and tells you that race, gender, and age have been studied, so Choices A., B., and E. are out. The second paragraph states that "much research" has been done on the effects of witnesses who are asked misleading questions. A misleading question is a type of question, so you can infer that the effect of the question type on eyewitness accounts has been studied and cross out Choice

C.. You can reasonably assume that the amount of time that passes between an event and an eyewitness's account of that event would affect the accuracy of the testimony, but the question doesn't ask for your reasonable assumption. Because Passage A doesn't mention any studies conducted to see how time affects eyewitness testimony, Choice D. offers the exception. Remember to answer questions based solely on information in the passage, regardless of any outside or personal knowledge you may have on the subject matter.

15. **B. Eyewitness testimony is often flawed because it is influenced by a variety of factors.**

The best answer incorporates a point suggested by both passages. Eliminate answers that can be supported by only one of the passages. Passage A makes the statement that there's no difference between the accuracy of male and female testimony, but Passage B doesn't discuss the role of gender, so Choice D. is supported by only one passage and can't be right. Although both passages mention that eyewitness testimony is affected by a number of variables, only Passage B discusses the importance of determining an error rate. Passage A doesn't mention the establishment of an error rate for testimony, so you can't assume Passage A supports Choice E.. Neither passage discusses how memory improves or declines over time, so Choice

C. is out of contention. That leaves Choices A. and B.. Choice A. doesn't seem likely. The first line of Passage A states that "there are many factors that may account for mistaken eyewitness identification" and then goes on to describe the research of these factors, which implies that mistaken eyewitness identification occurs frequently enough to warrant significant study. Passage B stresses the science of memory and human cognitive abilities and states that they're "not perfect." In the third paragraph, the author of Passage B points out that establishing an error rate

involves an awareness of the many factors that affect eyewitness accounts. Neither passage suggests that eyewitness testimony is "highly" accurate, but both imply that accounts may be flawed by the influence of several factors or variables. Because it's a better answer than Choice A., Choice B. is correct.

16. **A. How the lighting in a particular event affects the reliability of eyewitness identification is a variable that warrants a good amount of study.**

Your job is to eliminate reasonable implications of Passage A. The passage tells you that one's race can affect how well one recognizes someone's face, so it implies that one's race may adversely affect the reliability of an identification. Cross out Choice B.. The passage justifies the statement in Choice C.. It categorizes the factors as system variables and estimator variables. So Choice C. is wrong. The passage states that the majority of research has gone into studying system variables, and the makeup of a lineup is a system variable. So you can reasonably infer Choice D. from the statements in Passage A. The passage tells you that the way questions are worded is a system variable, and the judicial system has control over system variables. Therefore, the author of Passage A must think that the judicial system has control over whether a witness is asked misleading questions. Because Choice E. is wrong, Choice A. must be the answer. Passage A states that lighting can affect an eyewitness identification, but because lighting is an estimator variable over which the judicial system has little control, it's unlikely to receive much research. The passage states that system variables receive the majority of study. The best answer is Choice A..

17. E. to understand how memory and human cognitive abilities are affected by a variety of different factors

Both passages discuss memory and how it's affected by different factors; what differs is the factors they discuss. Passage A covers variables that include the age, race, and gender of eyewitnesses and the wording of the questions they're asked. Passage B emphasizes the complexity of memory and cognitive abilities. Rule out choices that pertain to one passage but not the other. Choice A. is a concern of Passage B but isn't mentioned in Passage A, so it's wrong. Choices C. and D. are important to Passage A but not to Passage B. Choice B. isn't a goal of either passage. Though

Passage B does indeed mention episodic memory, aside from defining the term, the passage doesn't show how the concept contributes to judicial proceedings. By process of elimination, the best answer is Choice E.. Both passages deal with the complex factors that affect cognitive ability and memory as they relate to the accuracy of eyewitness testimony.

18.D. Both passages concern improving eyewitness accuracy, but Passage A focuses on controlling variables and Passage B concentrates on understanding the science behind human recollection.

You can eliminate some answers quickly because they aren't true. Choice A. is wrong because Passage B doesn't discuss witness questioning and therefore doesn't dismiss its importance. Choice B. isn't right because how the judicial system controls certain variables is a concern of Passage A, not Passage B. Eliminate Choice E. because both passages deal with how research can improve eyewitness accuracy: through research of system variables for Passage A and the establishment of an error rate in Passage B. Choice C. may be tempting because Passage A mentions the effect of race on eyewitness identification, but the way the question is worded implies that Passage B does indeed discuss race, at least to some degree, which is inaccurate. Choice D. is the only option that appropriately defines a noticeable difference between the content of the two passages. The primary focus of Passage A is the variables that affect the accuracy of eyewitness identification. Passage B is more concerned with the workings of the human mind and how this knowledge can be used to establish an error rate for witness testimony. Choice D. is best.

19. E. Lighting issues and the length of time someone witnessed an event are examples of system variables.

This question asks you for the statement that isn't supported by either passage. Eliminate answers that appear in either of the two passages. The second paragraph of Passage B states that the Daubert case argued for the need of an established error rate, so Choice D. is easy to eliminate. Choice A .is a premise of both passages; they both state that human memory doesn't get it right every time. Passage B says that eyewitness memory should make "guilty people seem more likely to be guilty," and Choice C. seems to paraphrase that statement. Passage B's first paragraph states that cognitive abilities are incredible and supports that statement with the assertion that visual, auditory, olfactory, tactile, and taste information

synchronizes with past information to bring that information into the present, so the statement in Choice B. is supported by Passage B. If you thought Choice E. was supported by Passage A, you confused system variables with estimator variables. Lighting issues and the length of time someone witnessed an event are actually examples of estimator variables. Choice E. is the answer that neither passage supports.

20. C. the philosophical origins of public schools in 18th century Germany and the transformation in educational thinking in the 19th century

This passage is about the origins of public education and the changes that occurred in educational philosophy in the first century of public schools; the whole thing is set in Germany. Choice A. doesn't cover the whole passage; the political message seems to apply only to the first half. Choice B. also focuses on just the first half and so isn't the passage's primary point. The final paragraph doesn't focus on exploitation at all. Choice C. conveys the passage's overarching theme. Choice D. is wrong because the passage doesn't get into modern educational practices. Choice E. doesn't cover the whole passage, just the first part of it. Choice C. is correct.

21. C. They were indifferent to the well-being and needs of their workers, caring only to maximize production and profits no matter what it cost their employees. The author tells you that textile mill owners exploited their workers badly enough to incite revolts and that they embraced the concept of schools in the hopes that it would make the workers more docile. Choice A. is quite wrong. The first schools weren't created to help the students

so much as to help the nobles. Choice B . could well be true, but the passage doesn't discuss it. Remember, all correct answers must not stray too far from the text. Choice C . fits well with what the passage says about the owners. It does appear that they were indifferent to the well-being of their workers. Choice D . isn't quite right. The passage doesn't specifically tell you that they were all aristocrats. Although some of them may have believed their authority was divinely ordained, you can't assume that was true of them all, nor is there any reason for you to assume that they cared about nurturing their workers. Choice E . is wrong. The passage doesn't contain anything about the factory owners being patriotic. Choice C . is the best answer.

22. B. Eighteenth-century schools were concerned primarily with teaching working-class children to accept their fate and love their ruler; 19th-century schools began to focus on developing the full human potential of students. The educational difference between the two centuries was philosophical. Schools in the 1700s were meant for workers and intended to instill patriotism and gratitude toward the government into their students, but schools in the 1800s aspired to develop children to their full potential. Choice A . isn't right because 18th-century schools had nothing to do with efficient textile mills. Choice B . looks like a very good answer. Choice C . doesn't work because 18th-century schools were for the children of workers, not the aristocracy, and in the 19th century, no one had to spin anymore. Choice D . is tricky because it's very close to being correct, but the passage doesn't tell you that 19th-century schools aspired to create free-thinking students in general (though academic freedom was prized for advanced students), so it's wrong. Choice E . may actually be true — it sounds like some parents of Spinnschulen children didn't like the schools if truant officers were necessary — but that's not the main difference between the centuries, and the passage doesn't really address this point. Choice B . is the right answer.

23. A. riots and other forms of violence against the owners of textile factories by peasants unhappy at their treatment. Look at the sentence after the one that mentions increasing levels of unrest. It says that the rulers wanted "to channel the energy of restless peasants into something that would be less dangerous to the throne than riots." So "unrest" must mean riots and other violent uprisings by workers who disliked their lot in life. That would be Choice A .. None of the other answers work. Choice E . is tempting because it concerns young people, and this passage is about schools, but the statement doesn't restrict the violence to young men. Choice A . is correct.

24. E. They liked the idea because it would make the peasantry more complacent and acccpting of their fate, which would help keep the aristocracy safe in their

prosperity. According to the passage: "Aristocrats liked this idea. They liked the thought of schools making peasants more docile and patriotic, and they appreciated the way state-run schools would teach children of lower social classes to accept their position in life." Choice A. is wrong because the schools were intended to do just the opposite; educating workers was supposed to make them more docile, not more violent. Choice B. doesn't work because the passage never mentions aristocratic resentment of taxes. Choice C. may be a true statement, but the passage doesn't directly come out and say it. You know nothing of the aristocratic opinions of Schlabrendorff himself. Choice D. is wrong because the passage doesn't tell you that the education would be specifically religious. Teaching children that their "lot was ordained by god" doesn't mean that the entire curriculum was religious. Choice E. is the most suitable answer to this question.

25. B. to take away the authority of parents and replace it with state power over children and citizens. The truant officers were meant to take away parental authority over children and replace it with state control. Choice B. is the most accurate answer. The truant officers weren't there to make sure every child was educated, so Choice A. is wrong. They didn't help or indoctrinate parents or children, nor did they recruit boys into the army, which nixes Choices

C. and D.. Though they may have indirectly assisted the king and his administration in the compliant-citizen project, which would make Choice E. a possible answer, but it's much less specific than the answer given in Choice B.. Choice B. is best.

26. D. People learn best in an environment that respects their individuality, affords them freedom, and incorporates a variety of aspects of learning, such as physical movement, manual skills, and independent exploration.

Nineteenth-century educational theorists believed in nurturing innate abilities and using holistic techniques. That's not Choice A.. In fact, Choice A. is just the opposite of what experts thought in the 1800s. Choice

B. is wrong because nothing in the passage mentions religion. Choice C. isn't right. The passage never suggests that the state has an interest in an educated citizenry, just an interest in a docile and patriotic one, and that wasn't the prevailing view in the 19th century anyway. Choice D. looks like a perfect answer to this question. Choice E. isn't right because the passage never mentions that mothers were good teachers for their own children. That makes Choice D. correct.

Section 4 Writing Sample

Of the two communities, Brookville would better serve both of the Dawsons' objectives.

With respect to their first objective (reducing living expenses), Brookville is far and away the better alternative. By moving to Brookville, the Dawsons could apply a significant portion of their home-sale proceeds toward funding their retirement, whereas in Haven Hill they could not. Moreover, their property tax bill would probably be higher in Haven Hill.

Even aside from housing costs, resort communities are notoriously expensive places: restaurants are often upscale and pricey, and products such as gas and groceries often cost more because tourists are willing to pay more and because the costs to transport to these isolated spots are greater. The main recreational activity in Haven Hill, skiing, is notoriously expensive as well. By contrast, the sorts of amenities that Brookville has in spades — for example, bike paths, a good library, and an adult education program — are all either inexpensive or free.

Turning to the second objective, the Dawsons might find Haven Hill's local arts scene and Swanson College's performance program and art gallery equally attractive. However, Brookville holds more potential in terms of the entire array of cultural opportunities available to the Dawsons — who after all seek to enjoy their golden years largely by engaging in as wide a variety of cultural activities as possible. A good library is a cultural cornucopia, and the extension courses that Swanson now offers will in all likelihood serve to round out the Dawsons' continuing cultural education nicely.

Moreover, should the Dawsons seek other cultural activities — ones not available in Brookville — a major metropolitan area is only a short drive away. Haven Hill is far too isolated, and since it has no college or university and no continuing education courses for older adults, the Dawsons may soon tire of Haven Hill's local arts scene and find themselves culturally isolated and starved.

As for recreational opportunities, of the two choices Haven Hill might seem to have more to offer: skiing, hiking, and fishing. Yet it is entirely possible that Haven Hill is too crowded during the winter for the Dawsons to enjoy skiing on a regular basis, and they might soon grow to old or frail to ski or, for that matter, to go on rigorous hikes up and down mountain slopes. Leisurely strolls and bike rides around a college campus might very well suit them better, especially over the long term.

In summar, the Dawsons should move to Brookville because of the two choices it better meets both of the Dawsons' objectives. Owning a condominium and living in Haven Hill might very well drain them financially, while the more affordable Brookville would provide the broadest possible array of the sorts of cultural and recreational activities that the couple not only would like to but would be able to enjoy for the rest of their lives.

Made in the USA
Monee, IL
13 May 2020